ACKNOWLEDGEMENTS

Many people and organisations have helped us with this study. First we must thank the Joseph Rowntree Memorial Trust which funded the project and its staff, especially Richard Best, Robin Guthrie, Janet Lewis and Jane Morton. We also received much valuable support from the Advisory Group which the Trust appointed to assist us. Jane Dibblin, our editor at Shelter, did a magnificent job in helping us to put the final text into readable English and spotting several ambiguous or inadequate passages.

A second debt of gratitude is owed to our consultants whose role is described in an appendix at the end of this book. They were Peter Marcuse and Chester Hartman in the USA; Jos Smeets and Helga Fassbinder in the Netherlands; and Ruth Becker, Klaus Novy and Friedrich Malz in West Germany. Particular help was given in the USA by the Community Information Exchange, whose work is discussed in chapter seven. The exchange generously allowed our US consultants and ourselves free access to its computer based inventory of innovatory housing projects. In addition, Trevor James assisted greatly with the Dutch projects.

Further support for the project was provided by the Economic and Social Research Council which funded the 1986 seminar at which the preliminary results of our work were discussed (see appendix II for further details).

Finally, we must thank all those, too numerous to list here, who took time off from working on the projects which we visited to answer our questions.

Michael Harloe   Maartje Martens
Colchester   Amsterdam

February 1990

Michael Harloe is a Professor of Sociology and Dean of Social Sciences, University of Essex. He is a member of Shelter's Board of Management and was formerly adviser to the House of Commons Environment Committee and to the Secretary of State for the Environment. He is the author of several books and articles on housing and urban development, including **Housing and Social Change in Europe and the USA** (Routledge, 1988) which he co-authored with Michael Ball and Maartje Martens.

Maartje Martens now works for the Housing Research Institute, University of Delft. She was formerly the Senior Research Officer at the Department of Sociology, University of Essex. She has also worked as a housing researcher for FNV (Dutch trade union federation). She is the author of books and articles on housing, including **Housing and Social Change in Europe and the USA**.

Contents

1. The Importance of Innovation

This book reports on some innovatory housing projects which have recently been developed in the United States, West Germany and the Netherlands. We hope that it will interest those who are concerned about British housing, whether they are in the public or the private sector, whether they are responsible for providing housing or represent housing consumers. Immersed in the day to day problems of housing, there is an understandable tendency to concentrate only on the next issue to be resolved. But this all too easily results in blinkered vision when important issues concerning the future of British housing and the prospects and possibilities for change have to be considered. As we will argue in this first chapter, a cross-national study of housing innovations can help us to break out of such a restricted view.

The need for a broader view of the future of British housing is especially important now. With a whole range of policies since 1979 culminating in the 1988 Housing Act, the present government aims to bring about a radical and highly controversial series of changes in housing, particularly in relation to the housing of lower-income households. These changes present a particular challenge to their critics to come forward with their own new ideas and a new vision of the future of British housing.

In various localities up and down the country, new developments in housing are now occurring. Some of these have influenced government thinking, others have been promoted by those who are highly critical of government policies. New developments involve, for example, the devolution of management responsibilities to tenants, so-called 'new forms of tenure' and the attempt to develop public-private sector co-operation. Similar experiments are occurring in other countries and we hope to show in this book that we can benefit from learning about some of the positive and the negative features of these foreign innovations.

In this chapter we look in more detail at the value of cross-national studies of housing and explain the particular significance of a comparative study of housing innovations at this time. Then we discuss how we selected certain innovations for study. Finally we provide some information about the housing situation in the three countries where our research was carried out. A note on how the research was done will be found in appendix II.

The value of comparative housing studies

In the last decade housing, like much else in British society, has gone through a remarkable series of changes. Ten years ago, who would have believed that in 1988 a derelict cottage measuring 25ft by 25ft in Gloucestershire would have been auctioned for £181,500; or that in 1989 one of the largest building societies would be trying to turn itself into a bank; or that the private landlord would be rescued from the grave; or that council housing might soon fade away into insignificance?

Many housing practitioners and consumers have little opportunity or apparent reason to spend time thinking about just why these changes have occurred. The more pressing problem is to cope with their consequences. Politicians have a greater interest in providing explanations of change but these, with few exceptions, are fairly superficial. Most debate takes place within the narrow and distorting limits set by party political conflicts, in which the assignment of blame or credit for what has occurred is of paramount importance.

The House of Lords debate on the second reading of the 1988 Housing Act provides a typical example of this. For the minister introducing the bill the changes occurring in British housing were the product of a government which, for the past ten years,'*has been freeing our country from a mass of obsolete controls and outdated thinking*' and was following a '*coherent policy*' which would '*tackle this country's housing problems effectively*'. For opposing peers this policy was nothing more than a '*fraud*' which '*offers little hope for the future*'. However, whatever the evaluation of change both sides saw it as '*an inevitable outcome of government policy*' (Hansard, House of Lords, 11 July 1988, cols 596-681).

Clearly, most of the argument is over housing policies. These are seen as the determinants of who gets what housing and how much they pay for it. But most British housing is provided and financed by the private market. Of course, housing policies affect how this market works but they do not control it. To give one example, the radical changes now occurring in how building societies operate – some of which have helped to fuel recent house price inflation and put home ownership beyond the reach of many households – have been encouraged by government policies and changes in the law. However, these new policies have followed – not led – the changes in national and international financial markets which resulted in increased competition for savings and investment and higher interest rates.

A good way of beginning to understand how current changes in housing are brought about by more than just the recent actions of the British government – important though these are – is to survey the contemporary scene elsewhere. However, with few exceptions, there has been a lack of serious interest in, or knowledge about, what is going on beyond these shores.

References to foreign experience have tended to be brief, typically being used by those who are arguing for or against particular British policies. For example, in the House of Lords debate referred to above, a government supporter claimed that the experience of France and West Germany in maintaining a substantial private rented sector demonstrated the value of the government's attempt to resurrect this tenure in Britain. Equally, opposition peers who wished to argue the case for public sector housing referred to the success of the Scandinavian countries in this respect. But these are hardly more than debating points, the selective and often misinformed appeal to whatever aspect of foreign experience seems to support the case being made.

However, we can learn a good deal and deepen our understanding about what is happening to housing by looking at contemporary developments elsewhere. Let us return to the example of mortgage finance. Despite the widely varying ways in which home buyers obtain loans in different countries – and the extent to which governments try to control this – the economic pressures for the type of reform of the building societies now occurring in Britain are virtually universal. So even a brief study of foreign experience helps to direct our attention to the crucial importance of general economic trends, such as the internationalisation of financial markets, which have at least as much impact on the prospects for British homebuyers as anything which the government does by its own efforts.

Therefore, understanding the wider context within which housing policies operate, and which often determines whether they achieve their objectives, is one valuable contribution which comparative studies can make. We can also use such studies in a quasi-experimental way as a means of highlighting the possible consequences of new policies now being implemented in Britain.

The 1988 Housing Act aims to follow the example of countries such as Germany, the Netherlands and France by basing most social housing provision on independent landlords, leaving councils with the overall responsibility for housing conditions in their areas. Such landlords are seen as less bureaucratic than local authorities and inherently more responsive to tenants' needs. But if one seriously examines social housing in the above listed countries one soon discovers that many of the same criticisms that have been made of council landlords in this country are made of independent social landlords abroad.

Moreover, there are new problems which occur when the political responsibility for housing conditions is separated from direct access to a source of housing supply. Many local authorities in the countries mentioned have found it difficult to get social housing allocated to those in the greatest housing need because independent landlords shy away from housing those whom they regard as 'problem' households.

Once again, some real knowledge of the foreign experience can contribute to our understanding of the British situation. In this case, even those who support the dissolution of council landlordism might have their attention directed to some of the key problems which their preferred policies will have to resolve.

So international comparisons can help illuminate what really determines why British housing is the way it is and what new problems are likely to occur with changes in the way our housing is provided. But can they also help us to arrive at better ways of dealing with these problems? Can they provide new solutions?

We are not entirely optimistic about this because of the 'translation' problem – the difficulty of applying the lessons of one country to another. Recently there has been some interest expressed by British policy makers in gathering information on specific foreign housing policy developments with a view to their possible implementation in Britain. Two transatlantic examples which have had an impact are urban homesteading and tenant management.

But sometimes the 'research' into such foreign developments has been little more than information gathering about their immediate details. There is little attempt to assess whether – or how – they can be 'translated' from one nation to another, given the considerable differences in the economic, social and political context which are likely to exist between the two countries concerned. Of course, the importance of such differences soon becomes apparent when such innovations are tried out. But a clearer understanding of how they operated in their country of origin would often have helped to prevent subsequent difficulties.

These differences imply that the search for policy 'blueprints', ready-made solutions which can be imported wholesale, rarely has much value. Individual housing markets and policies are shaped not only by a combination of broad socio-economic factors, which to a great extent they share in common with other countries, but also by their individual histories, politics, and social and organisational structures. What we can most usefully do, when searching for positive lessons relevant to our own policies, is to focus neither exclusively on the detail of foreign housing systems, nor solely on the broader common factors which affect many such systems, but on what lies between these two levels of understanding.

What this means can best be illustrated by returning to the example of tenant management. Succesful tenant management schemes have been implemented in a small number of American public housing projects. The details of how these schemes operate are somewhat different in each case, depending on local circumstances. At the same time, a set of extreme circumstances, brought about by the way in which US public housing is organised and financed, exerted intense pressure on all the tenants of these schemes to take up self-management.

In some cases, had they rejected this option they would even have lost their housing. In any foreseeable British situation where tenant management was a possibility it seems unlikely that the threat of eviction would provide the main motivation for tenants to act. So one factor which accounts for the success of this development is irrelevant in the British situation. This should militate against any simplistic view on the possibility of transfering US tenant management schemes lock, stock and barrel.

The US experience teaches us not how tenants can be induced to take over their management but, rather, particular lessons in cases where there is some desire by tenants for self-management. We might want to know more from these examples about the relationship between the prospects for self-management and the degree of tenant turnover or the level of management training required. In particular, if we are able to examine several broadly similar policy developments involving tenant management, occurring in different cities or even in different countries, we will have a clearer idea of the common problems they encounter, how they have been resolved and how we can apply this to our own situation.

In this book we have just this aim. We are not presenting a ready-made set of 'solutions' to the problems of British housing. This would be a futile and misleading objective. We do believe, however, that especially at a time of rapid change in British housing, it is important to break out of narrow and parochial thinking through comparative studies.

We will focus on a particular selection of housing innovations in three countries. Many of the innovatory developments we discuss are, as yet, on a small-scale and in this sense are relatively unimportant. However, there is a particular significance to the study of housing innovations at the present time. To explain this further we have to look at the broad context within which the housing markets and policies of Britain and many other countries are now operating.

Recent changes in housing markets and policies

Before discussing the significance of housing innovations, we briefly summarise some key aspects of the general changes now occurring in housing provision. We have written about these in detail elsewhere (see Ball, M., M. Harloe and M. Martens, *Housing and Social Change in Europe and America*, Routledge, 1988). Our conclusions are based on extensive research carried out over the past ten years in Western Europe and the United States.

This research has shown that, with the collapse of the long post-war boom and the accompanying political consensus (or at least compromise) over the extent and nature of state involvement in economic and social processes, some radical changes in housing provision are occurring. These are more than simply incremental adjustments to altered circumstances.

Six major aspects of change are important:

▶ The circumstances of owner-occupied housing markets have changed in the last decade. Despite short term fluctuations, house building has been in secular decline. Housing markets are now much more unstable and sensitive to general economic changes. The real cost of house purchase has increased since the 1970s and is unlikely to return to the low levels of that decade.

▶ One major reason for this situation is the dramatic changes which have occurred in mortgage finance. Semi-protected and rather low cost circuits of housing finance have been breaking down and there has been an increasing integration of housing finance into general financial markets. Funds are now more expensive and more volatile; flowing into and out of the housing market according to its profitability with respect to other investment opportunities. Volatility and high costs help to perpetuate the instability of owner-occupied housing markets.

▶ Unstable housing markets have had profound effects on housing production. In some countries large-scale builders have almost disappeared, in others, they have become more dominant. But a common feature is that, whilst the building industry may be becoming more concentrated in some cases, large-scale structures of building organisation and management are giving way to smaller scale, more flexible and fragmented arrangements. Housing developers now have to pay far more attention to marketing their products, to seeking out profitable sub-markets and sectors of demand.

▶ Social rented housing production has been radically cut back by governments of the left and the right, sometimes simply to reduce public expenditure, sometimes – as in Britain – because they are ideologically opposed to it. A trend towards limiting social housing to those excluded from the private market because of their incomes and social situations is also apparent. Rents have risen sharply at a time when tenants' incomes have only been growing slowly and income-related housing allowances have not fully compensated for this. Also, social segregation within social housing is increasing. 'Problem' estates are developing, where there are concentrations of socially and economically disadvantaged households.

▶ Rents have also escalated in private rental sectors and, in many cases, conditions for low-income households living in such housing have deteriorated. New investment is very restricted. New building is rare unless substantial direct or tax-based subsidies are available for investors. Even so, the rents of these units are often too high for lower-income households. They are mainly built for limited sub-markets of more affluent, young and mobile households. Improvement investment is also linked to such sub-markets and often results in gentrification and the removal of lower-income tenants. Meanwhile, landlord disinvestment in unprofitable lower-income rental housing has continued. In the United States this has even taken the extreme form of landlords abandoning their properties on a large scale.

▶ Despite much cross-national variation in housing policies there are some common trends. All governments aim to reduce public housing expenditure. In some cases, the rationale is purely macro-economic; in others, governments also believe that state involvement in housing is socially damaging. However, there is considerable resistance to some aspects of government cutbacks. For example, many governments would like to reduce tax subsidies for owner-occupiers but are frightened of the possible political fall out. But the pattern and role of government support is changing. Increasingly, government assistance is directed to supporting the private market provision of housing while support for social housing is being cut. A central dilemma – only dimly recognised, if at all – is that this is being attempted at a time when there has been a decline in the ability of the private market to provide decent yet affordable housing for broad sections of the population, at least without continuing major state support. And yet it is just this commitment which governments wish to reduce.

These changes in housing markets and policies have not, of course, affected all households equally. Large sections of the population, especially those who remain employed, continue to be reasonably well housed. They may pay rather more for their accommodation, or accept a lower quality of housing. They may become involved in new forms of housing provision, perhaps, because otherwise they can no longer afford the standard of accommodation that they have come to expect or because traditional forms of provision do not suit their particular needs. But the process of adaption to change has not been severe compared to that experienced by lower-income households.

Lower-income households have been most seriously affected by the reduced availability and higher costs of housing. Promises made during the post-war boom to end shared accommodation, substandard and deteriorating property, insecurity of tenure, homelessness and excessive housing costs are no longer being met. In every country which we have studied, there is a growing mass of housing disadvantage and stress for such households, while conditions for those whose economic security is relatively assured because of their position in the labour market and the benefits that they still get from housing subsidies, have improved.

To summarise: the past few years have seen many changes in the relatively settled pattern of housing provision which developed in the post-war era and which for many years was rather successful in achieving a steady improvement in housing quality and affordability for the majority of the population. New problems of housing supply and affordability are arising, or rather, old problems are being resurrected, to which the established system of provision has no answer. In this situation the importance of focusing on innovations arises, for these are often attempts to find new solutions to new problems.

The contemporary significance of housing innovations

We will outline some of the main areas of innovation below but first it is interesting to note that, when viewed as a whole, these innovations also reflect some broad shifts in political and social ideas about housing. These ideas began to change in the 1970s, particularly in response to a growing critique – from the left and the right – of the bureaucratic, paternalistic and rigid structures of social housing. The right was also critical of almost any state involvement in welfare, believing that market-based provision was inherently superior. This belief in the free market is, of course, not shared by left wing critics but what both left and right do share is a greater interest in concepts of self-help and self-reliance. However, for the right this self-help is seen in individualistic terms. In contrast, the left tends to stress collectivist forms of self-provision and organisation.

This growing emphasis on self-reliance also reflects changing attitudes and spending power among some housing consumers. Some sections of the middle class (including those, such as groups of young people, who may be poor but in terms of their origins and education have a middle class background) now have different attitudes regarding the desirability of

14

'conventional' living arrangements, for example. And these groups have also faced growing housing costs and difficulties of access to housing, though much less severely than the poor. These are some of the reasons why they have become involved in collective schemes such as co-operatives.

On occasion, the impulse towards change has come from a different direction. Some housing developers and financial institutions are interested in introducing more consumer participation into their developments as a way of opening up new markets.

Although many of these innovations are, as yet, of marginal quantitative significance, some have been enthusiastically promoted by housing related institutions and governments, often with words if not with much money. Such projects are often held to illustrate the merits of private initiative. However, there is frequently a degree of tokenism involved in this promotion. The existence of small-scale innovatory projects, most of which are relatively cheap to finance, suggests that these institutions and governments are concerned with meeting housing needs and are actively seeking new and more effective ways to do this. At the same time, major housing programmes which had much more quantitative significance in the past continue to be cut back.

The selection of innovations for the study

The academic and management oriented literature on innovation is full of discussions about what counts as innovation. Is it something which is entirely new or is it simply new to the type of organisation, community or whatever, in which it occurs? In this book we take the latter view. (Some economic historians usefully coined the term 'derivative innovations'). This means that some of the projects which we describe will not be entirely new to our readers. For example, we shall discuss the development of 'mutual housing associations' in the USA. These are strongly influenced by the long-established housing associations of Western Europe. Nevertheless, there are some aspects of the way in which the associations are being established which differ from the European model and which are of considerable interest. Our principal concern is to contribute to thinking about innovatory developments which may already be underway by providing information about parallel developments elsewhere, not – in most cases – to suggest that wholly novel experiments are going on elsewhere. In practice, this is simply not the case.

Another recurrent issue in the literature on innovations concerns the way in which it implies that all innovations are positive developments almost by definition. However, there are some innovations which we shall ignore. One

15

of the consultants who helped us with this study, Peter Marcuse, has named these 'reverse innovations'. A good example is the growth of inadequate forms of housing 'solutions', such as doubling up, living rough or in hostels and night shelters (in what have recently been called 'non-tenures'). Here we are only concerned with innovations which are, at least, potentially positive solutions to the types of housing need which are decreasingly satisfied by 'conventional' provision.

We are also less interested in what Marcuse has called 'defensive' innovations. This is where one section of housing consumers innovates to sustain its own access to housing at the expense of another, less well endowed group. The classic example is gentrification and the accompanying displacement of lower-income households. In fact, we shall mainly be concerned with innovations which at least purport to offer some benefits to lower and moderate-income households, those who have been hardest hit by contemporary problems of affordability and supply.

A final consideration in selecting the projects to be discussed was the degree to which they had some wider relevance beyond their country of origin. Some innovatory developments are so closely tied to the specific local or national context in which they occur that they are of little practical interest outside this context.

We have chosen to group the projects according to six themes. These are:-

▶ New forms of social ownership

▶ New management structures in social housing

▶ New ways of funding lower-income housing

▶ Extending home ownership

▶ Self-help in design and construction

▶ Organisations supporting housing innovation

One problem with this method of organising the material was that individual projects often qualified for discussion under more than one of these headings. However, we have allocated projects to individual chapters on the basis of what appears to be the most interesting aspect of their innovatory character and have only referred to them more briefly in other chapters where appropriate.

A second problem was how to present the enormous amount of material which we have obtained on the 50 or so projects which we examined in detail. Rather than provide a lengthy and indigestible catalogue of every project, which would also be superficial and of limited value, we have focused on a limited number of projects which are of particular interest, referring to other examples of the types of innovation which we are discussing more briefly. The major projects which we examined, together with a brief description of their nature, are listed in appendix I to this book, in the order in which they first occur in the chapters. Our aim is to draw out some of the key lessons to be learnt from these projects rather than to provide information about every detail of their structure and functioning. As we have already argued, to do the latter would not be an appropriate or very useful exercise.

One final problem concerns the presentation of financial information about the projects and those who live in them. We have chosen not to convert figures which are expressed in dollars, deutsch marks and guilders into their sterling equivalents because we believe that this is a fundamentally mistaken approach. Such translations encourage the reader to make direct comparisons between foreign and British situations which can be misleading, given the wide differences which exist cross-nationally in relation to matters such as housing costs, income levels, the contribution made by state subsidies to lowering housing costs and the proportion of income devoted to housing in comparison with other expenditures.

However, Table 1.1 provides some data on approximate exchange rates and earnings for the period just before the research was carried out. It illustrates the need to avoid simplistic financial comparisons, given the wide gap which now exists between British levels of earnings and those in the other three countries.

Table 1.1

Exchange rates and earnings
Exchange rates
£1 = $1.63; 2.93 DM; 3.3 guilders

Average hourly earnings in manufacturing industry and indices

United States £5.85 (100)

West Germany £5.53 (94.5)

Netherlands £4.90 (83.8)

United Kingdom £3.70 (63.2)

Sources: Eurostat 7, 1989; UN statistical yearbook 1985/6, 1988.

The housing situation in the three countries

We have already set the broad context, in terms of changing housing markets and policies, within which the innovatory projects that we will be considering operate. But some further brief details about the current situation in the three countries is also necessary. Our choice of the Netherlands, West Germany and the United States was based on the findings of previous research. This had shown that there were particularly interesting projects in these countries which would be worth a closer examination. However, our selection of countries was also governed by several other pragmatic considerations, such as the availability of locally-based expertise to help us with the research.

Notable features of the three housing markets include;

▶ The very different size of the three housing markets and the varying significance of the main tenures (see Table 1.2 which shows the position around 1980). The private housing market is most clearly dominant in the USA where the public housing stock is very small scale, although it is much more significant in some of the big cities. In addition, about two to three per cent of the private rented stock has been aided by direct federal government subsidies and might be regarded as a form of quasi-public housing. Private rental housing is particularly important in Germany, where it has been extensively aided by government. But in both Germany and the Netherlands owner occupation grew very rapidly in the 1970s with much government support.

Table 1.2

Housing tenure as a percentage of the stock around 1980				
	Netherlands	Germany	USA	Britain
Social rent	43	18	2	31
Private rent	13	45	32	11
Owner-Occupied	44	37	66	58

Source: M.Ball et al., Housing and social change in Europe and the USA, 1988

▶ The recession in the late 1970s and early 1980s seriously affected private building. A downward trend in new house building from the peak levels reached in the early seventies occurred in each of the three countries. Declining levels of building for social renting were especially apparent in

Germany and the United States. In the Netherlands social house building increased for a short period in the early 1980s when a serious collapse of the private housing market forced the government to revert to its earlier anti-cyclical public investment policies.

We detail below the organisations responsible for the provision of social rented housing in the three countries. In all cases, these organisations have some degree of independence from central or local political control. General political responsibility for housing is differently located in the three countries. The role of the Dutch government in housing comes closest to the British case. In Germany and USA, the federal governments have a more limited involvement in housing and both state and local governments have more autonomy and more responsibility. In Germany, the role of the states is particularly important, in the USA much less so.

USA: Public housing is developed and managed by about 2,800 public housing authorities. These are legally autonomous public corporate bodies, created by local government according to state enabling laws and run by commissioners. They are often strongly influenced by local politics. Funding is by tax-exempt bond issues. Federal subsidies cover debt servicing and some operating costs; modernisation subsidies have also been provided. The authorities are subject to detailed federal regulation. The average stock holding is around 450 units (many are not run by professional staff) but about five per cent of the authorities manage two thirds of all public housing.

Netherlands: Since the 1960s housing corporations have been the main providers of social housing, rather than local authorities. They can build for all tenures but any 'profits' have to be reinvested in housing. They are subject to government and local authority regulation, although there is a continuous struggle to retain some autonomy – especially from the local authorities. They can take two forms, membership associations and foundations, the latter having a managing board and no members. Most now take the first of these forms. They receive government subsidies and various forms of assistance from local authorities. They usually only operate in one local authority area. There are about 900 corporations with an average stock holding of around 1,400 units.

West Germany: The situation is complex. Social rented housing has been provided by 'non-profit' organisations, private individuals and companies, within general rules set by government regarding standards, rents and tenant eligibility. 'Non-profit' landlords are limited to a dividend of four per cent. Many have strong links with the local authorities. They take various legal forms, including co-operatives. These are membership-based and usually fairly small, other 'non-profits' are often managed in a highly bureaucratic and centralised way. Many only operate in one locality but some have developed on a far wider scale. All social landlords are eligible for subsidies, mainly provided by the federal and the state governments. Social landlords which are not 'non-profit' have the right, eventually, to sell off their units or let them at market level rents. Recent legislative changes will result in the loss of much of this part of the social stock to the private market by the mid-nineties.

Finally, it is also useful to consider some brief details of recent policy developments in each country:-

The United States: As in Britain, public expenditure on housing has been one of the main casualties of a central government committed to New Right policies. On coming into office in 1981, President Reagan aimed to terminate federal support for new low and moderate-income housing (but not support through the tax system for middle- and upper-income housing). Early indications are that the Bush administration is unlikely to reverse this policy trend. However, Congressional resistance has prevented the complete ending of federal support and, in particular, some resources have been available to meet the operating costs of existing public housing and allow it to be modernised. There is also a declining programme of income-related subsidies ('housing vouchers') to allow low-income households to rent basic quality housing in the private sector, although the widespread existence of discriminatory letting practices and lack of suitable vacant properties often prevent eligible households from obtaining accommodation.

The federal government also provides a Community Development Block Grant to localities, some of which is used, at the discretion of the locality, for assisting lower-income housing. Apart from tax subsidies for owner-occupiers, much like those which exist in Britain, there are some tax shelters available for investment in lower-income housing. These will be discussed later in the book. In addition, there are a variety of local and state programmes which aim to increase the supply of affordable housing. These include loans with favourable terms, some direct subsidies and tax (including property tax) remissions. Most of this assistance is aimed at encouraging private investment in low to moderate-income housing, not expanding publicly owned supply.

West Germany: After the collapse of the centre-left government in 1982, the centre-right coalition under Chancellor Kohl has sought, as have President Reagan and Mrs Thatcher, to reduce the federal government role in low to moderate-income housing and to stimulate the private market. This has had an important impact on social rented housing and on rent levels. New legislation has modified Germany's system of private sector rent regulation and has increased problems of affordability. Because of the way in which rents are set in the social housing sector acute problems of affordability are also apparent here, especially in the expensive housing built in the 1970s. But the most serious result of policy changes is that from 1987 the federal government was no longer willing to provide subsidies for the building of social rented housing, although they are still available to subsidise some housing built for owner occupation. These changes mean that new additions to the stock of social rented housing are dependent on the willingness and ability of the states and local authorities to provide assistance.

In addition, about 50 per cent of the existing social housing stock will be freed from rent and other controls by the mid-nineties and will be available for letting at market rents or for sale to owner-occupiers. This will especially affect the social stock which is owned by private landlords (social subsidies have been available for non-profit and commercial landlords). Moreover, in a further move to reduce state support, in 1988 the government withdrew the privileged tax status of most non-profit housing. In future, only co-operative housing will retain this benefit. At the same time, successive governments have extended support for home ownership. As West Germany is a federal state, lower tier governments can have some policy leverage but can, at best, delay the process of privatisation which is now occurring.

The Netherlands: The centre-right governments in power in the Netherlands during the 1980s also wished to reduce public expenditure on housing. However, for a variety of reasons housing remained a sensitive political issue and direct government support is still extensive, at least, compared to many other countries. This support is provided not just for social rented housing but also for most private market construction. However, the radical cutbacks in expenditure which have occurred in Germany, the USA and Britain emerged as a feasible option for Dutch governments in the mid-eighties, when the private housing market made a limited recovery from its earlier collapse. The cuts led to a decline in new social rented housing and there was a considerable increase in social and private sector rents. These increases are determined by central government. Its aim has partly been to reduce the rapidly growing burden of housing subsidies in the national budget. In addition, the government no longer provides loans for social house building and improvement. This has increased debt charges and, hence, rents.

New directions for Dutch housing policies were outlined in a White Paper published in autumn 1988. Subsidies are to be targeted on lower-income households. It is likely that this will undermine the 'general needs structure' which has previously characterised Dutch social housing. At the same time, tax subsidies for owner occupation have been maintained, although some cuts will be made in the variety of direct subsidies which exist for new building for owner occupation. Changes are also foreseen in the institutional structure of the housing associations. These may inhibit the scope for innovation. The private character of the associations will be emphasised, the new formation of associations severely restricted and concentration and centralisation encouraged. Along with a more professionalised management will go greater financial independence from government. This means that investment risks will be transferred from the government to the associations – and ultimately to the tenants. Further proposals, which include narrowing the associations' role to only housing those with low incomes, will have profound implications for tenants and for relations between local authorities and the associations.

There are some important general consequences of these recent developments in the three countries. First, the attempt by central governments to reduce their role in supporting low- and moderate-income housing is placing greater pressure on local and state governments to fill the gap and to search for new sources of finance in order to achieve this end. In some cases, it has also encouraged them to re-introduce controls over the private sector to ensure that some stock is reserved for lower-income households, for example by rent or allocation controls.

Second, the reduction of government subsidies, plus the much higher real cost of housing in the 1980s due to historically high levels of real interest being paid for housing finance, means that problems of affordability are affecting a wider range of households than in the 1970s. These are, of course, most severely felt by socially and economically disadvantaged groups but more generally many new entrants to the housing market find that they have to pay very high levels of rent and mortgage charges and their access to reasonable housing has been greatly reduced. At the same time, attempts are being made to reduce the extent of income-related housing allowances to offset the rapid escalation in such expenditure which has occurred as housing payments have risen faster than recipients' incomes. This exacerbates the problems caused by the declining supply of new housing which can be afforded by lower-income households.

Third, one response to the increasing problem of housing affordability is the search for a means of reducing the cost of housing. There is pressure to reduce the standards of new housing and also to limit housing improvement to the minimum. In addition, self-help is often regarded as one promising way of reducing costs. There are also some attempts to reduce the cost of housing finance by rescheduling the pattern of loan repayments.

Finally, there are some major demographic and social changes which are also affecting housing policies and markets. In particular, there is the trend towards smaller households. This is due to changes in birth rates and an increasing proportion of elderly households but also factors such as increasing divorce and family breakdown and more children leaving home at an earlier age. A significant proportion of these smaller households are woman-headed with low incomes which add to the demand for cheap housing.

Changing household structures require a rethinking of the type of housing that will be needed in future. Smaller households do not necessarily need smaller houses but perhaps different types of houses. The standard single-family house does not, for example, necessarily cater for the needs of the elderly – either in terms of its internal planning or in relation to its location. Among the young, there is a demand for housing which is suited to new patterns of living, for example, in dwelling complexes with some communal facilities.

Several of the innovative projects which we discuss in this book are responses to the increasingly diverse pattern of life styles which recent social and demographic changes are helping to bring about and which the existing stock, built at a time when the main demand came from families with children, is ill-adapted to meet. To some extent, governments and the private market are responding to these demands – see, for example, the growth of group dwellings for the elderly – but only to a limited degree.

2. New Forms of Social Ownership

As we noted in the last chapter, the long established forms of social ownership of housing have been subjected to increasing criticism from the left and the right in recent years. Although there are widely differing conclusions drawn by these critics, social landlords are commonly seen as too remote, bureaucratic, inefficient and unresponsive to tenants' needs. We also noted in the last chapter that severe cuts in new social housing investment have been virtually universal and in some countries, such as Britain and West Germany, important steps have also been taken to privatise the existing stock.

However, as we shall see later in this book, there are severe limits on the extent to which private market provision, can take the place of social housing, at least without heavy subsidies. However, some developments are potentially a more positive response to the criticisms of existing social housing and to the current attempts to reduce the stock of such housing. In this chapter we discuss several projects which involve innovative forms of social or collective ownership. In the next chapter we discuss innovations in the management of existing social housing.

Some of the types of innovatory developments discussed here have also been pioneered in Britain. But, following the 1988 Housing Act, alternative forms of social ownership have become a far more significant issue than hitherto, so the comparisons as well as the contrasts provided by foreign case studies are likely to be of value. In this chapter we examine three particularly innovative projects, one from each of the countries, and consider several others more briefly.

Collective forms of ownership in West Germany

The forms of social or collective ownership which now exist in West Germany have links with earlier self-help movements in housing. The tradition goes back to the late nineteenth century when the lower middle classes formed building and saving associations, like the British building societies, and industrialists and the upper middle class encouraged workers' self-help building associations. Many new self-help initiatives emerged during the years of the Weimar Republic. Such housing policies were, in part, seen as a way of diverting the revolutionary threat posed by mass unemployment. As housing capital was in short supply, self-help was seen as a partial substitute.

The requirement to contribute ten to fifteen per cent to the cost of new social housing (both for rental and owner-occupation) as a downpayment or in the form of self-help has continued after 1945. However, instead of collective ownership and control, post-war governments have encouraged individual ownership while transforming the social rented sector into one dominated by centralised, bureaucratic and undemocratically controlled housing corporations. Interestingly, some of these trends were prefigured by Nazi policies from the early 1930s.

However, now a new wave of collective self-help initiatives is emerging in West Germany. Compared to the earlier period, self-help now has more to do with maintaining an existing low cost housing stock than with new building. The large-scale inner city squatter movements of the 1970s were in the vanguard of such initiatives. Debates over alternative forms of tenure developed more seriously in the 1980s, when the Wohnbund (which we discuss in chapter seven) became an important national force supporting new forms of collective ownership. The necessity for such experiments has grown with the increasing privatisation of the traditional social rented stock. Here we discuss two examples, the first located in prosperous southern Germany and the second in the declining industrial Ruhr region.

Neighbourhood Development Foundation – Hessen

The Stiftung Nachbarschaftliche Träger, which translates as Neighbourhood Development Foundation, was established in the summer of 1986 with support from the local state of Hessen, in Central Germany. It aimed to develop housing which would remain permanently in social ownership and could not lose this status as a result of government action. Furthermore, the housing would be tenant-managed. The ending of federal subsidies for new social rented housing raised two issues for advocates of social housing. First, the need to find alternative sources of support for investment in social housing and, second, the need to organise the ownership of such housing in ways which ensured that it remain permanently within the social sector and available for low-income households.

The opportunity for some action on these issues opened up in Hessen, which had long been a stronghold of the Social Democratic Party and whose governments had, therefore, actively supported social housing. From the 1970s onwards, the Green Party began to make inroads in the SPD vote and after state elections in 1983, the Social Democrats could only retain power by forming a so-called Red/Green coalition government. While the Social Democrats supported 'old style' social housing, the Greens favoured decentralisation, self-management and radical reforms in the operation of social housing.

It was in this situation that some ideas, previously developed by housing researchers and activists, got taken up by the new coalition government which was searching for a housing policy acceptable to both its constituent elements. The researchers and activists were particularly interested in reviving some of the socially progressive features of the small, self-organised working class housing co-operatives which had been founded in the early twentieth century. In addition, Eberhard Mühlich, a housing researcher and one of the key movers in the setting up of the foundation, had made a detailed study of the recent co-operative housing developments in Liverpool and wanted to transfer some of the lessons of these developments to Germany.

Mühlich told us that the argument put forward for setting up the Foundation started from the realisation that as a high level of unemployment and the growth of low wage employment seemed likely to continue, there would be a persisting need for social rented housing in Germany. However, funds were unlikely to be available for much new social house building. In any event, new building would be too expensive (the problem of high rents and lack of affordability of recently built social housing is acute in Germany and is not fully relieved by the system of income-related rent allowances).

The solution was to obtain much cheaper stock by buying up privately rented property in the older urban areas and rehabilitating it. This would have several other advantages, in particular, it would inhibit the spread of gentrification which was reducing the stock of cheap housing in many cities. Also, some groups in these areas, such as young people and possibly communities of guest workers, might be prepared to form organisations to own and collectively manage such housing.

This form of decentralised housing provision would be cheaper to rent and more democratically controlled by its residents than traditional social housing. However, if tenant groups were not assisted they would find it very hard to obtain the necessary finance for their projects, so some form of central organisation was required to provide funds for the local projects. This was the role of the Foundation which would obtain finance to support various forms of collectively owned and run social housing.

In an attempt to guarantee its continued existence whatever future changes in government policies might be, Mühlich and his colleagues argued, successfully, that the Foundation be established as a 'public right' foundation. It was a tax-free non-profit entity with a set of objectives related to the provision of social housing. According to the law under which it was established, it could not be abolished, even by subsequent government legislation, unless its objectives had been entirely realised. However, as we note below, it was soon found to be vulnerable to action against it by a hostile government, partly because it remained dependent on government funding and partly because of the way in which it was structured.

The Foundation had two governing boards which were mandatory under German law. One exercised overall control on policy matters and one was an executive body. But the Foundation had a third board which had the right to initiate all project funding proposals which then went to the other boards. This board represented as directly as possible the types of community based housing projects which it was established to aid. Groups which wished to develop such projects were invited to nominate board members. The other boards were filled by a wide range of people, including representatives of the political parties, housing researchers, a banker with housing interests, an official of the state housing ministry and managers of existing social housing organisations. New political representatives would be nominated after each state election but the other members were appointed and replaced by the boards themselves.

The Foundation was endowed with a 10 million DM capital grant from the state government. This guaranteed it a continuing income which would pay for its core staffing and other running costs. To support specific projects it had to obtain funding from the state housing ministry. In 1987, at the time of the research, an annual budget of up to 45 million DM was available for this purpose, subject to the Foundation being able to recommend projects which the ministry would approve for funding. In the long term its initial capital, and hence, its scope for operations, would be augmented by revenue from the projects which it supported (see below). It was envisaged that the Foundation eventually would become a self-sustaining revolving fund, but this would take a long time to achieve.

The state project funding was not to be used to meet the full costs of projects. Instead, it would enable the Foundation to buy the land on which these projects were located. The Foundation would then lease the land to the tenants. The building work would be financed by a mixture of low interest loans or grants from the Foundation plus commercial loans. Its retention of the land enabled it to ensure that the 'social' character of the projects was secured through special clauses in the land lease which defined matters such as the requirement to house certain types of households, to set rents at the minimum necessary levels and to manage the properties in certain

28

ways. Such conditions were established as a result of private contracts, so they could not be abrogated by government action. If tenants broke the lease conditions the whole project would revert to the Foundation. The agreements were to run for 99 years.

Projects had to fulfil a number of key criteria to be accepted for funding. First, they had to mainly serve households within the federal government's income limits for access to social rented housing (this covers about fifty per cent of the income distribution) although, because many projects would involve already occupied housing units, there was some latitude in this respect. Projects with the lowest income households would get the highest priority. Second, the housing had to be available at a price which allowed any necessary repair/improvement work to be done and rents to be set at affordable levels (note that tenants were eligible for federal rent allowances but there are limits on the absolute levels of rent which will be subsidised).

Third, the location and circumstances of projects would be important. For example, a project in an area where gentrification was occurring and where the maintenance of a supply of low-income housing was important, but was under threat, would be a high priority for funding. Fourth, the availability of a group of lower-income households with the ability and willingness to undertake self-management was important. Finally, where possible, the Foundation wanted to encourage projects which would also expand local employment opportunities, for example by combining accommodation with space for small businesses.

Rents would be set at locally comparative market levels for tenants who could afford them. Other tenants would receive income-related rebates. The aggregate rent roll would determine how much money could be privately borrowed at commercial rates to fund the project. The Foundation's provision of low interest loans or grants would complement this funding. In some cases, it would also reduce or waive the ground rent it charged the tenants for up to 10–15 years until, with falling historic costs, the rents covered costs. The Foundation staff knew that they would be able to get private finance for the projects provided that they were economically viable. They also expected tenants to contribute some resources via private loans, for example, from relatives.

All the housing was to be rented and self-management was essential. The Foundation did not intend to become a large-scale, bureaucratic landlord. At the same time it was recognised that extensive training would be required if tenant management was to work. So money was earmarked for this purpose. It was estimated that 10 to 20 per cent of the Foundation's funding would be used for training. The form of self-management, whether, for example, to have paid staff or to rely on voluntary labour, would be for the projects to decide.

There were many issues which could only be resolved in practice – for example, concerning how and when the Foundation should intervene if conflicts occurred between the tenants. However, the Foundation would set rules for, and check on, their financial affairs and had set some basic rules for tenant selection. Eighty per cent of all tenants had to have incomes within the federal government social rented housing limits. Forty per cent of vacancies had to be let to households nominated by the local authorities from their lists of those in urgent housing need. Following a common practice in German social housing, the local authorities would put forward three names for each vacancy and the tenant managers would select one. Sixty per cent of vacancies would be allocated by the tenants' own organisation. There was some concern about possible bias and discrimination in selection but, rather than increase centralised control to avoid this, the Foundation hoped that any problems could be resolved by discussion and education.

There were several possible sources of cheap properties which the projects would require if they were to produce affordable housing without the normal social subsidies. For example, some landlords who wished to sell off their property for speculative purposes (for conversion to owner-occupation) might face tenant resistance and be prepared to sell to the Foundation at a reduced price. In other cases, property might be obtained from social landlords, although the Foundation was reluctant to acquire these. There were also redundant commercial buildings which could be converted for low-income housing.

At the time of our research, the Foundation was just beginning to identify projects suitable for its support, although it had already become involved in one project which concerned the takeover of a social housing estate (see below). Gert Behrens, a Berlin lawyer who had acted as the director of a company that had managed legalised squatting in that city, had been hired to direct the Foundation. He told us that 27 projects had been considered so far and six or seven of them seemed viable. These included a project in Frankfurt involving young unemployed people who wanted to buy a house and renovate it using job creation funds; an old factory in the small town of Giesen which a young printers' collective wanted to convert for housing; and a seventeenth century building – which had been a hotel and later a doctor's practice – which a group of skilled workers wanted to convert. All were on a fairly small scale.

The main obstacle to progress was not the financial soundness of the various projects but the degree of preparedness of the tenant organisations concerned. Behrens felt that the sort of grassroots community-based organisation which was common in American cities was much less well developed in Germany, where there was a strong expectation that the state would provide housing and other welfare services and, as he said, '*people are used to being administered by others'.*

The Heimat Siedlung – Frankfurt

In a rather unplanned way, responding at short notice to an emergency situation, the Foundation had already become involved in the tenant takeover of a large social housing project. This is the Heimat Siedlung, a very well known housing project in Frankfurt designed and built in the 1930s by Ernst May, a leading modern architect of the period. Situated just off a busy main road near the centre of town, the housing is built round a pleasant garden square. The project is very much in the style of the Modern Movement: low rise, balcony blocks, designed in a simple yet elegant manner, with white painted concrete facades and small apartments with rooms which are carefully oriented to catch the sun wherever possible. Even though it is now over 50 years old this is still basically very good housing, in a convenient location for access to the town centre. The housing had been owned by Neue Heimat, the trade union backed housing association which had been the largest social landlord in Germany.

However, Neue Heimat had recently collapsed and efforts had been made to sell off its housing stock in order to meet the huge debts left by the organisation. There has been a good deal of conflict over these sales, with tenants resisting the possible loss of their housing when the properties are sold to private investors. This seemed the likely fate of the Heimat Siedlung but there was a small group of tenants on the estate who wanted to establish a co-operative to buy the properties. According to Hannelore Schneider, a local community activist who lived on the estate and was one of the group, they requested the aid of the Foundation in early 1984, just as it was being set up.

Rents on the estate were already quite high because of recent improvement works. Some 40 million DM in debt plus the running costs needed to be covered by rents which were at 6 DM per square metre, close to the maximum rent level set, through rent-controlling legislation, by the city council. This limited the scope for a private buyer to raise rents and increase the project's profitability. Such profits could be made by piecemeal sales for owner-occupation but this could only occur slowly, when vacancies arose. In any event, many of the tenants were elderly and could not afford to buy or to pay greatly increased rents. It was to prevent hardship and the possible displacement of such tenants that the Foundation agreed to support the purchase of the estate from Neue Heimat, despite the fact that this was a much larger scale operation than it normally intended to become involved in (the estate has 1,072 dwellings).

After some bargaining the project was bought for 79m DM. Affordable rents levels were calculated. These were higher than before as they had to be related to the purchase price. In the event, these rents would cover running costs plus a 30m DM fixed interest loan at the normal commercial rate. The other 49m DM required for the purchase was provided by the Foundation. Of this 49m DM, 44m DM comprised the land cost and the extra 5m DM was an interest-free loan. An annual ground rent was payable to the Foundation but this was capitalised for reasons that will be explained below. It was calculated that after 22 years the commercial loan would be paid off, then the co-op would start paying off the interest-free Foundation loan. After 50 years all the debts would be repaid. Then, according to German co-operative law, the co-op could sell off the buildings and distribute the proceeds to its members. However, the capitalised ground rent would equal the likely value of the buildings after 50 years, so there would be little incentive for the co-op to sell out.

To form the tenant co-operative it was necessary for each household to buy a share in the organisation (thus providing the co-operative's own, small, equity in the project). This amounted to three months rent but because sitting tenants could choose whether or not to join the co-operative (there was no question of their being evicted if they chose not to) this 'own capital' could only be built up over time, although all new tenants would have to become members of the co-op.

The Foundation believed that the housing which it supported would be far less costly than conventionally financed social housing. For example, at the time of our research new social housing units cost 2–300,000 DM (building and land costs are far higher in Germany than in Britain or the other countries in this study). In comparison, the cost of the Heimat Siedlung was about 80,000 DM per unit.

However, as already noted, the most difficult aspect of the Foundation's work concerned the establishment of tenant self-management, not the financial details of the projects in which it was interested. This was borne out by Hannelore Schneider's account of the problems which the tenants' group had faced in the Heimat Siedlung. Because of the urgent necessity to secure the future of the project it had to be bought before the co-operative could be established. As a temporary expedient the project was being managed by a Heimstatten (a type of social landlord sponsored by the state government). When we visited the project in 1987 a paid manager had just been hired by the tenants and the group of active tenants were trying to persuade all the other residents to join the co-operative.

Schneider told us that a few tenants were strongly resisting this. Rather more would agree to join but were reluctant to contribute, in practice, to self-management. Fifty per cent of the tenants had to agree in order to set up a co-operative; by early 1987 this point had almost been reached. Attendance at general tenants' meetings was fairly good – about 150–300 people turned out – but few tenants attended the meetings of the tenants' elected executive, to which all could come, or had shown much interest in training for self-management.

In short, tenants still needed to be won over to the idea of co-operative organisation and self-management. Hannelore Schneider told us, 'some are very confused and think self-management means that they have to carry out work themselves, rather than hiring staff. Many think that the co-operative is, in the circumstances, the best solution to their problems but for purely pragmatic reasons. Only a few see it as more than an economic solution, as something which has a wider political and social significance, which shows that tenants can do things for themselves and become a local political force'.

In fact, many tenants strongly rejected this view, feeling that any such political role, even if in the tenants' own interests, was a 'dirty business'. Most tenants were fairly passive, going along with decisions which were largely still being taken by the small group of activists that had originally fought for the preservation of the Heimat as social housing.

However, it should be remembered that the Heimat was not typical of the sort of projects which the Foundation was really established to support. And the Heimat's activists had discovered that tenants on other local social housing estates, used to low rents and a reasonably effective 'traditional' social housing management which had done little to consult or involve them, were also rather passive and disinclined to form their own organisations to press for their interests.

The Foundation mainly intended to work with groups which had developed some level of activism and commitment before seeking its support and who wanted to take over private housing and other property. For these private sector tenants, in contrast to those in social housing projects such as the Heimat, there was no history of low rents and/or reasonably effective, if paternalistic, management.

The lessons of the Heimat Siedlung experience are, however, of considerable relevance to the development of self-management in existing social housing – a topic which we shall discuss in the next chapter.

The Rheinpreussen Estate – Duisburg

The experiences of the tenants of this estate contrast interestingly with those of Heimat Siedlung. Here, tenants fought hard to establish a co-operative. The Rheinpreussen tenants were strongly working class and about 35 per cent were foreign workers, whereas the Frankfurt project had more middle class occupants.

The estate is located in Duisburg, in the Ruhr near the border with

It was built as a garden city by a mining company at the turn of the The houses are very small – most buildings contain four units. After changes in ownership in the 1960s, it was bought by a building ny which demolished 1,200 units and replaced them with high-rise . After this company went bankrupt in the early 1970s, the project was taken over by a bank which wanted to demolish the remaining 600 original units, replacing them with luxury bungalows.

The tenants organised to resist this. After an 11 week vigil outside the bank's headquarters and the town hall, they won. The town council declared the estate an urban renewal area, thus preserving its housing and making it eligible for subsidies. After the bank tried to sell off units individually, the rest of the estate was bought by the council, with support from the state, in 1979.

Because the area had been affected by uncertainty for so long, the buildings were very run down and expensive repairs were necessary. In order to use urban renewal subsidies the properties had to be transferred to private ownership again. Several options were discussed. The main ones were resale to an existing housing corporation or a tenant co-operative. Eventually,the tenants voted, by a quite narrow margin, for the second option. The co-operative was formally established in May 1984.

The average income of a four person family on the estate was 1,750 DM per month. It was agreed that rents should, therefore, not exceed 4.35 DM per square metre. The price for each dwelling including improvement costs was set at 57,000 DM. The state provided 46,000 DM, using urban renewal funds. The remaining 11,000 DM was to be funded by the co-operative. Half this was to be provided in the form of help in carrying out the repair work and the rest was to be borrowed commercially. Rents included a ground rent paid to the council at a fixed level for 66 years.

Not all the tenants had chosen to join the co-operative – those who were not members did not contribute work hours but had to cover the whole 11,000 DM by increased rent payments. However, tenant solidarity was such that the self-help contribution of able-bodied members of the co-operative was increased by 20 per cent to cover the costs of improvements to units occupied by the elderly, disabled and single mothers. The average self-help contribution, for the whole project, then amounted to 150 hours, which the tenants called a 'muscle mortgage'.

The rent also included a 0.20 DM per square metre 'solidarity contribution' to fund new building. This was a requirement of the legislation regulating social landlords. Initially, these funds were to be spent on improvement works but by the time that these were finished in the late 1980s there was expected to be about half a million DM available for new building.

A full-time and part-time manager were hired, out of the rent income, to

run the project. While the improvements were being carried out two architects were also employed to supervise the self-help work. These were
organised on a collective basis and the task of the co-operative was to
provide the organisational framework for democratic decision-making and
work-planning.

Maatschappelijk Gebonden Eigendom – Rotterdam

Maatschappelijk Gebonden Eigendom, 'socially bound ownership', is a
pioneering project that aims to provide social housing which is owned by its
occupants rather than rented. These occupants have many of the benefits
of individual home ownership but in a form which prevents the property being
resold on the open market and being lost as a source of accommodation for
moderate-income home buyers. It involves, in effect, a new form of tenure,
akin to co-operative housing but organised on the basis of individual rather
than collective ownership.

The project began in the late seventies. According to the city officials we
interviewed, Rotterdam had a socialist council for many years which
supported social rented housing and looked for alternatives to home
ownership. However, there was growing criticism of this policy, so the
council began to look for ways of supporting a form of socialised ownership.
Like many localities in the Netherlands, the local authority exercised strong
controls over the type of housing built in the city because it owned most
development land. Its policy was that this land should remain in public
ownership so that the benefits of rising land values should accrue to the
community, not to private interests. Therefore, most development took place
on land leased from the council – a requirement for any new policy towards
owner-occupation.

Another factor also influenced council policy. A major house price boom
in the late 1970s encouraged many financial institutions, insurance companies for example, which had large holdings of private rented flats to sell off.
As in London, many of these sales were to speculators who specialised in
the break up of the estates and their resale for ownership or for rental to
higher-income groups. This policy was resisted by many tenants' groups.

Earlier, under the leadership of an energetic local councillor, Alderman
van der Ploeg, Rotterdam council had carried out a very controversial
municipalisation policy, taking much of the poorer housing owned by smaller
landlords in its inner areas under its wing (van der Ploeg simply threatened
the landlords with the rigorous enforcement of local housing regulations if
they did not sell up). The problem was that this had placed a very large
financial burden on the city due, not so much to the cost of acquisition, but
to the costs of the necessary repairs and improvements.

In the late seventies, the city considered whether it could convert some of this property to a form of socially-controlled owner-occupation but the costs of bringing the housing up to a reasonable standard meant that it would be too expensive for the current low-income tenants to buy their homes. Another way of developing the new form of owner-occupation would be to build so-called premium housing, new housing aided by direct government subsidies for moderate-income ownership. However, the city could not impose conditions ensuring that such housing remained permanently available to moderate-income buyers because similar housing could be bought without such restrictions in other localities.

The city concluded that the housing being sold off by the institutions offered the best chance for creating the socially controlled owner-occupation which it wanted to develop. The officials showed us some pictures of this property. It was very different from the inner city near-slum housing which van der Ploeg had municipalised. Most of the housing had been built between the 1930s and the 1950s for renting to middle class families. With the exception of a few houses, there were mostly flats in a wide variety of shapes and sizes, ranging from one and two bedrooms up to five or six bedroom units. Most were in low rise blocks in the more attractive inner suburban areas.

The properties were in a fairly good condition, some had been built pre-war but many, more recently. Moreover, as one official told us, '*many of the institutions were embarrassed by the conflict over their sale to speculators, so they sold us the estates at a lower unit price than if they were sold separately for ownership or for renting to the better off*'. Interestingly, the city retained a British co-ownership housing expert to advise them. But there were legal restrictions and a lack of familiarity with this form of tenure in Holland, so the city decided to use several housing associations as its agents in converting the properties to socially controlled ownership.

The properties were bought by the city at their investment value for about 13 times the annual rent roll (and most rents had been kept at a fairly low level). The plan was that around five per cent of the units would be sold to individual owners each year. The city resold the housing to the associations, retaining ownership of the land. The price paid by the associations, which used commercial loans to make the purchases, was fixed so that the rent income plus the income from the assumed rate of individual sales would just meet the debt repayments.

The sale price to individual buyers was supposed to be set at 60 per cent of open market value. It was estimated that the restrictions which were put on the resale of the properties, to ensure that they remained available for moderate-income buyers, justified a 40 per cent discount. In fact, various additional costs meant that, in practice, the price was somewhat higher. The scheme was arranged so that the associations would break even after 10-15 years and would then make some profit which they could use for other housing purposes.

Apart from their mortgage repayments, the buyers pay a ground rent to the city; an annual contribution to an external maintenance fund (which is run by the association and the homeowners, each having voting rights based on the size of their holdings); and an administration fee to the association. It was calculated that the full costs of owner-occupation would only be a little above current rents and, given future rent rises, within a few years buying would be the cheaper option.

Apart from the sitting tenants, new buyers have to have initial incomes which are within the limits for access to social rented housing. In addition, when the owner wants to sell, he or she has to sell it to the housing associations. The price is based on the original low sales price with an allowance for subsequent inflation based on changes in the consumer price index, not the house price index (which was rising more rapidly at the time when the scheme started).

At the same time, there is a deduction for depreciation, equal to 1.2 per cent a year of the original sales price. If significant improvements have been carried out by the owners this is taken account of in determining the resale price, as is any abnormal deterioration of the property. These restrictions allow the units to be resold to moderate-income households at affordable prices. The original buyers have the initial value of their investment protected (less the depreciation allowance) but are not able to make larger capital gains by selling on the open market.

In practice, few of the sitting tenants, many of whom were elderly, wanted to take on ownership responsibilities. So they opted to continue as tenants. Most sales were of vacant units. Households with the lowest incomes (under 20,000 guilders per annum), including families on social security or unskilled workers, could not afford to buy. The housing was sold to skilled workers and younger office workers earning around 30–40,000 guilders a year (the limit for social housing eligibility at the time was around 40–50,000 guilders, depending on family size). Normal mortgages were easily obtained, as resale at a price which would more than cover the initial loan was guaranteed. The average sales price was about 60,000 guilders and total payments around 320 guilders a month (compared with average rents of around 290 guilders).

The officials told us that many young couples have bought because the payments were little more than they would have paid in rent and their mortgage repayments allowed them to accumulate a little equity which could later become the downpayment for a conventionally owned suburban unit. They described the scheme as 'a bridge between renting and buying'. The city did not advertise the scheme widely but there was a strong demand for it, although this varied according to the attractiveness of the location of the properties.

The city bought just under 1,900 properties between the late 1970s and the early 1980s. But the scheme ran into difficulties. By the time we did our research no new purchases were being made but the council was restructuring the programme so that it could continue. The most serious problems were financial. These were caused by the collapse of the housing market and of prices in the early 1980s, which we referred to in the last chapter, plus rapidly rising interest rates and housing association rent rises (set by national government for all housing associations) which failed to keep up with the increasing loan charges.

On the one hand, this meant that the deficit before taking account of sales proceeds was far higher than had been forecast. On the other hand, the higher interest rates and depressed prices adversely affected the sales revenue. The costs of the purchasers' loans increased sharply while, if they remained as tenants, they only paid rents which were increasing at a slower rate. This discouraged sitting tenant purchases. In addition, falling real house prices discouraged other households from applying to buy. Moreover, as prices plunged in the free market they came closer to the sale prices of the scheme's units. In the first year of the programme the volume of sales exceeded the predicted five per cent, it was about 12 per cent. But it then fell very rapidly, as hardly anyone wanted to buy the units.

The housing associations faced financial disaster and the city council had to rescue them. The units were taken away from the associations which had managed them and became the only stock owned by a housing association, set up by the city, which would mount a professional and well managed sales campaign. One problem had been that the associations had many other rented properties and had not given sufficient management attention to dealing with their social ownership stock. This transfer allowed the original associations to pay off their debts. The new association was able to buy the units with new bank loans contracted at seven per cent. The original loans were at 12 per cent, so the economics of the scheme improved. At the time of the research, the scheme seemed to be financially viable again.

Just under a third of the units had been sold over a six year period, thus meeting on average the annual target for sales. But there had been no new purchases since 1983, despite some offers of properties in that period. The city was looking at how the scheme might be expanded. This was not easy as most of the housing which had been owned by the institutions had been sold. For the scheme to work, the property acquired had to be in basically sound condition but available at a reasonable price. This ruled out new housing development and also the purchase of the older and cheaper but dilapidated private rental housing still owned by many smaller landlords.

One possibility was the purchase of social rented housing from the housing associations, some of whom wished to raise money for much needed improvements and repairs to the rest of their housing (for which insufficient government funds were available).

The scheme was a unique experiment. There has been one other project in Zaandam, north of Amsterdam but this concerns 41 newly built units and the tenure is a co-operative form of social home ownership. The occupiers buy a right to use the units rather than property rights. Because these users have mortgage loans the development of their housing costs is somewhat more predictable (most mortgage loans in Netherlands are at a fixed interest rate) than in the case of social renting, which involves annual rent rises. Users are guaranteed not to lose the money that they have invested but cannot make speculative gains.

There has been some national political interest in promoting social home ownership for moderate-income households. A 1983 government discussion paper on owner-occupation mentioned the possibility of using the scheme for premium (directly) subsidised owner-occupation and recommended further studies. But there have been no further developments since this time.

Mutual housing associations – USA

The previous innovations discussed in this chapter are attempts to ensure a permanent supply of lower-income housing which could not be lost from the social sector, either by government action or by sales on the open market. This is also one of the main reasons for the development of mutual housing associations in the USA. These have been supported by the Neighborhood Reinvestment Corporation, an organisation set up by Congress in 1978 to support inner city revitalisation programmes.

Beverly Heegard, who was responsible for the Corporation's work with mutual housing associations, told us that the idea of establishing mutual housing associations had been discussed by housing activists for several years before the first projects were started. The Corporation had become involved because a Congressman who supported its work had seen German co-operatives when on a European trip and been impressed by them. As in Western Europe, there was concern about the likely decline of the existing stock of subsidised low-income rental housing. In the USA much of this housing was owned by private investors and was only subject for a limited period to controls which guaranteed lower-income occupancy.

Many of the units which were built in the 1960s and early 1970s were, by the mid-1980s, reverting to the private market. In addition, similar restrictions on the public housing stock were beginning to come to an end and some projects were likely to be sold off. Given the cutbacks in federal subsidies, there would not be significant additions to the stock to compensate for these losses.

The ideas behind the associations are loosely based on examples drawn from Western Europe and especially, West Germany. However, it is interesting to note that they conform more to the ideal of European housing associations than their actual practice, particularly in respect to their management.

The Reinvestment Corporation, a public non-profit corporation, had been heavily involved in supporting Neighbourhood Housing Services projects in inner city areas. These projects brought together local residents, financial institutions and city authorities to upgrade housing and local facilities in a concentrated area, the closest British equivalent being Housing Action Areas. These schemes placed a strong emphasis on encouraging home ownership as this was seen as an effective means of stabilising declining neighbourhoods (see chapters four and five for other programmes with this objective). The Reinvestment Corporation was concerned about the difficulty of extending lower-income home ownership in these areas because of sharply rising homeowner costs. Mutual housing associations were seen as a promising means of helping to achieve this objective.

According to Beverly Heegard, the Corporation was critical of previous federal programmes to expand lower-income rental housing, especially by means of tax subsidies for private investors. Too often such housing was inadequately managed and was very costly to develop. By the 1980s much of this housing was deteriorating. Often the original owners had defaulted on their loans. In some cases, the tenants were able to take over their housing. More often they lost their homes or the projects, if still sound, were sold off privately and rent and security of tenure controls were ended.

So the Corporation decided that a new way of providing lower-income housing was required. This housing should be permanently available for lower-income households. Furthermore, it should be owned and managed by an organisation which was committed to its permanent retention as social housing, not by one which was only concerned to ensure that it was a profitable investment. Some subsidies would be required but these should not be based on tax incentives for high-income investors. Instead, it argued, there should be an 'up-front capital grant' to reduce the initial cost of new and rehabilitated housing (rather like the British housing association grants).

These grants would be used to establish mutual housing associations which would develop, own and manage housing 'in the public interest', that is for low – and moderate – income households and on a non-profit basis. The associations would be partnerships between people seeking housing and people concerned with its provision. They would be committed to a continual expansion of their stock, using the assets which they created to provide the necessary resources. Their residents would have lifetime security of tenure.

The intention was to provide good quality but affordable housing. Members would pay an initial membership fee and participate in management and maintenance. The Reinvestment Corporation saw the associations as a tenure half way between ownership and renting, combining aspects of the residents' financial and maintenance responsibilities found in each of these tenures. The aim was that the associations should make use of a wide range of funding possibilities, involving grants and loans, to reach moderate and some lower-income households. Moreover, there would be opportunities to reduce costs by self-management and 'sweat equity' (self-building). In addition, they might be supported by charitable and socially oriented business organisations.

In the early 1980s, the Corporation began to establish a pilot association – the Alameda Place project – in an area of inner Baltimore where it had already been active and which had a community organisation that was eager to try out the concept. The project was to incorporate several key requirements. It should be a non-profit, publicly accountable organisation providing housing which local residents could afford. Its membership and Board of Trustees would consist of residents and those waiting for a house, community and local government representatives and professional advisers.

The organisation would eventually have a federal structure, developing individual projects and served by a paid staff. Residents and members on the waiting list and neighbourhood leaders would have the major voice in decision making but there would also be an input from the other groups mentioned above. Residents would pay a membership fee and a small additional amount which would be invested to provide some capital for replacement, modernisation and expansion of the association's stock. The members of the association would annually elect a Board of Trustees which would be responsible for the overall running of the association. However, each housing complex would have a council of its residents and other local residents. This would be concerned with management, maintenance and neighbourhood issues, would have its own maintenance budgets and take on some other management responsibilities.

In 1982 the Reinvestment Corporation secured a ten acre site for a 160 unit project. The site had long been vacant and was regarded as a local eyesore. A Board of Trustees was established and an initial 60 units began to be built. They consist of small, conventionally designed terraced housing with individual gardens. Because some local residents were suspicious of the development, believing it might become just another blighted and stigmatised low-income housing project, and because they wanted to

41

expand owner-occupation in the area, the association agreed to 40 units of privately owned housing being built by a commercial developer on the periphery of the site.

The development was financed by membership fees, a capital grant and private sector mortgages. Members contributed a fee equivalent to five per cent of the cost of the unit, about $2,000 to $2,500. This was refundable with nominal interest added if the member moved out.

Construction period financing was obtained from the state community development authority (using Community Development Block Grant funds), the city council and the Reinvestment Corporation. The permanent financing consisted of a capital grant which covered about 35 per cent of the project costs. This came from the Reinvestment Corporation, the state and city governments, corporate donations and about ten per cent of the total grant comprised members' fees.

The loan financing came mainly from tax free bonds sold by the city council but the hope was that when the project demonstrated its viability direct private sector borrowing could be substituted.

The first occupants of the Baltimore project were families with members employed full time in lower paid occupations, for example nurses, security guards and junior office staff. Without additional income-related subsidies these associations are too expensive for households dependent on welfare payments. Each applicant has to pay the membership fee on joining the association and then wait for a unit to become available. While waiting they participate in running the association, as do the other non-resident members of the association, such as community, civic and business representatives.

Heegard told us that one advantage of this structure is that 'waiting' members put permanent pressure on the association to expand its development activities and not become an organisation only functioning for the mutual benefit of its existing residents, a problem which has affected many European co-operatives. Waiting members have to demonstrate an active commitment to the project by attending meetings and participating before they obtain a unit.

Residents do not pay rent but a monthly membership fee, set annually by the Trustees. This covers mortgage, management, insurance and other costs plus a small contribution towards the association's reserves and a capital fund for further developments. In the Baltimore scheme the fee was about $250 to $350 per month, depending on the size of the unit. Members can nominate a family member as a first preference candidate to take over their unit if they move out or when they die.

The aim is to foster a sense of having a permanent stake in the project among its residents. This is well reflected in the comment of Shirley Allen, the association's vice-president, '*I feel the place is mine, I can live here as long as I please and if anything should happen to me, my daughter can stay here without any obstacles because it's written into our constitution that way'.*

At the time of our research in 1987, the Baltimore project was mid-way through its first phase of development and the Reinvestment Corporation was seeking to establish other schemes. There had been much interest in the concept of mutual housing associations and many community groups were submitting proposals to the Reinvestment Corporation for its support. These varied widely, some involved new building and some rehabilitation or the conversion of non-residential property. Some only involved a few units, others were on a larger scale. A wide range of financing mechanisms were being proposed, depending on the local possibilities. The Neighborhood Reinvestment Corporation was providing small-scale grants, averaging $25,000 each, plus technical assistance to see whether some of these proposals could be developed into viable schemes.

According to Beverly Heegard, *'mutual housing associations are not the only way of developing lower-income housing, nor are they viable in every area. One possibility which we are exploring is that there might be some cross-subsidy, with those on higher incomes supporting reduced rents for other residents'.* Self-help construction was also a possibility in some schemes. The Reinvestment Corporation's role is to assist local groups establish housing associations and monitor their early progress, providing help when difficulties arose. Like the Hessen foundation, it is strongly committed to withdrawing from an active role as soon as possible, allowing the associations to develop autonomously. In this respect, they are intended to have more independence from outside control than most European housing associations.

One of the most interesting features of the Baltimore project is that it has developed close links with other local residents and groups who are all committed to the revitalisation of their area. This wider role is stressed by Tom Adams, the Deputy Director for Field Operations of the Reinvestment Corporation, *'... we feel mutual housing associations could exert a tremendous stabilising effect on communities in decline'.* The experience of the association has also encouraged resident involvement in other local organisations, such as serving on school boards.

The project's housing is far better quality than the private units which local residents had insisted on being built. At the time of the research the owners of these units wanted them to be merged with the association. Beverly Heegard felt that most project residents had developed a strong identity with their housing and were participating in its management and in the design and planning of new facilities. Their right to hand their units on to their children is regarded as a very important factor in encouraging participation.

43

Other projects in social ownership

The projects discussed so far represent very different models for the development of new forms of social housing. Each is ultimately intended to operate on a fairly large scale. However, there are several other smaller scale projects which we visited which also have individual features of interest.

One is the Woonkollectief Purmerend, the Purmerend Housing Collective, a Dutch experiment in housing with an element of communal living spaces which combines rental and owner-occupied units. The scheme does not really involve a new form of social ownership – occupants remain either tenants or homeowners.

However, the novel feature, apart from the experiment in communal living, is that all subsidies are pooled, including tenant housing allowances and owner-occupier tax relief, to subsidise housing costs for those on the lowest incomes. The occupants have formed a type of co-operative association (which relieves them of any individual financial liabilities for the scheme) and are treated like any conventional housing association by the authorities.

Purmerend is a small town near Amsterdam which was designated as an overspill housing area for the city. Ron Somers, the secretary of the collective told us that local politicians were keen to develop plans which would make it a more attractive area. Their collective had grown out of a group within the local Labour Party who were interested in a form of collective living known in the Netherlands as 'central living'.

The 'central living' concept was developed in the 1960s and 1970s in response to the domination of family oriented forms of house building. It provides an interesting variation on communal living, as each household keeps a separate dwelling but shares certain facilities, with some activities organised communally.

The project consists of 71 newly built units. They consist of low rise blocks, much like many others in the Netherlands, constructed out of concrete panels but with a good deal of wood also used in the building. They are built round a garden square, all units either have a direct exit to this or a large balcony looking out over it.

Forty two of the units are social rented housing, which receives the normal subsidies; the others are conventionally financed owner-occupied units which receive direct premium subsidies under the general government scheme to support moderate-income home ownership. A wide range of income groups are housed on the site but half the occupants are unemployed, most of these are in the rental housing. There is also a wide range of household types and ages.

The complex is split into 10 groups of seven units each (the last unit is for a caretaker). Each has a communal space which mainly consists of a large kitchen and bathroom (there are also small kitchens and showers in each unit). The space had been provided within the cost and space limits generally applied to subsidised housing, so the private space and facilities had to be reduced inside each unit.

In the Netherlands the concept of 'central living' is much discussed, although relatively few such projects have actually been built. Most such projects have been in the social housing sector. Such schemes attract young people but also single older people and families where the parents have separated. The project contains many households with children; the possibility of shared childcare – or even the formation of a creche – as a consequence of communal living can be very appealing.

As already noted, the other innovative feature of the project is its financing. The housing allowances and direct (premium) subsidies for homeowners are paid directly into a central fund. The homeowner tax reliefs have to be individually claimed but are then paid over to the fund. Each household pays a fixed percentage of its income for its housing. At the time of the research this was 15 per cent plus one per cent for the communal space. Basic housing costs varied according to the size of the unit, so the pooled subsidies are used to meet the gap between these varying costs and the income-related housing payments.

About half the capital for the entire project was raised by the local authority (in effect about the same as the total cost of the social housing element) and the rest by a collective loan from a commercial bank. This finance loan covered all the project costs, including fees (unlike similar situations in West Germany, there is no requirement in the Netherlands for occupants to contribute a downpayment). According to the collective's officers, the main problem which the project has faced is to find suitable occupants to replace those who have left. New households have to more or less match those which have left – both in terms of size and income level.

MUSCLE (Ministries United to Support Community Life Endeavors) in Washington DC is an organisation which enables tenants to take over and rehabilitate their housing in a market which is subject to strong gentrifying pressures and where the supply of affordable housing is rapidly declining. MUSCLE – a church backed non-profit body founded in 1978 – acts as a development consultant, helping low-income tenants establish limited equity co-operatives. It also acquires vacant properties for rehabilitation and sale to lower-income households.

Under pressure from community groups concerned at the loss of affordable housing, the city council has passed some laws to inhibit gentrification. Among these is a requirement that before landlords sell their properties they have to give the tenants a first option to purchase by forming a co-operative.

45

The council makes some financial assistance available for this purpose. According to Alice Vetter, MUSCLE's Director, '...few tenants have the skills to establish a co-operative without considerable outside assistance. MUSCLE supplies this at far lower cost than private market professionals'.

As with the mutual housing associations, the objective is not just to provide decent and affordable housing but also, 'a process through which families and individuals faced with the uncertainty of displacement grow and gain security, as well as one which revitalises neighborhoods by developing quality affordable housing'.

Apart from forming the co-operative, MUSCLE has to survey the buildings, many of which require major works, and assess the cost of repairs. Most of the projects have involved very dilapidated ex-private rental and single family housing in run down, inner city areas (but not those which had gone beyond the point where they could be revived). At the time of our research, the smallest MUSCLE project had involved six units and the largest 95 units. If the project is viable, the co-operative has to obtain long term financing. Tenants have a year to get to this stage from the first notification that they have an option to buy.

At the time of the research the average cost of the units was between $25,000 and $40,000, including repair and improvement works. The city council provides various forms of assistance, including help towards the downpayment on the purchase (normally tenants have to contribute five per cent of the cost of their unit to buy a share in the co-operative), low interest construction period loans, help with the other costs incurred in co-operative conversion, and long term interest-free second mortgages of up to $16,000 per unit (or $20,000 in the case of very low-income households).

To obtain this long term finance, households have to have incomes of no more than 80 per cent of the area median (the eligibility level for federally subsidised low-income housing). To receive assistance from MUSCLE more than half of the tenants in a building must have incomes within this level. MUSCLE is one of a small number of similar organisations under contract to the city council to help tenants form co-ops and buy their homes.

Often the co-operatives obtain normal commercial loans for the first mortgage on their property. However, some banks have been reluctant to lend for such an unfamiliar form of housing. So an interesting method of obtaining the finance has been developed by adapting a commercial leasing procedure. A limited partnership is formed between the co-operative and several high-income individuals, who can obtain tax shelters for their other income by investing in the co-operative property. The outside investors put up most of the money; the co-operative only puts up 0.5 per cent of the cost and retains management control. The partnership lasts for a limited period, then the outside partners can be bought out by the co-operative.

Esther Siegel, who works for the National Association of Housing Co-operatives in Washington, told us about how this method of financing had been used to establish the co-operative in which she lived. When in late 1977, the tenants in her block of apartments had received eviction notices, they had organised to take advantage of the law which allowed them the first right to purchase. It was their financial consultant who came up with the idea of partnership financing, a method which has since been widely copied. In their case, the outside investors were bought out after six years.

It had been agreed that the increased capital value of the project over this period would be equally divided between the co-operative and the investors. This reduced the buy-out price below prevailing market levels at the time of the sale and, given rising incomes, meant that the co-op members could afford to buy out the partners with a normal commercial loan. Originally each member had invested $1,000 to buy a share in the co-operative, so creating its original stake in the equity.

In order to preserve the project for lower-income households it was agreed that this share would be linked to the Consumer Price Index, rather than to the far more rapidly appreciating level of Washington house prices. So when property became vacant it was still possible for less well-off households to buy the share of the departing household. This arrangement applied to the whole limited equity programme in Washington.

Discussion

In this chapter we have discussed a variety of new forms of social housing. Some, like mutual housing associations and limited equity co-operatives, are rather similar to parallel British developments. Indeed some of these initiatives have been strongly influenced by British projects, such as the Liverpool co-ops. In other cases, notably that of the Rotterdam social ownership scheme, the social sector is being extended in ways which have not, so far as we know, been tried elsewhere.

Many of these initiatives have faced considerable difficulties and not all have been a total success, often because they lack an established frame-work of political and financial assistance. We now discuss these difficulties in a little more detail, concluding with a reference to the crucial importance of 'enabling organisations'.

▶ **Financial problems** obviously beset many projects attempting to provide lower-income housing. But these are intensified in the case of innovative projects which many lenders view with deep suspicion. Thus the Rotterdam scheme required local authority mortgage guarantees to secure conventional financing. Similarly, the Baltimore housing association had to prove that it could work before obtaining private loans. Other problems include the downpayments in the German schemes, which restrict access except where households can substitute self-build contributions (see chapter six). On the whole, public subsidies are not nearly as generous as they might have been a few years ago, so there is a great stress placed on cost limitation and finding ingenious ways to combine various sources of finance.

▶ **Housing market developments** have sometimes aided the financial viability of projects. This was initially the case with socially bound ownership, where the difference between the sale price of the units and prevailing open market prices encouraged households to buy their units. However, before long the collapse in private market prices had the opposite effect and the scheme almost fell apart. The Washington co-operative partnership financing relies on the continuation of both rising house prices and incomes. So far this does not appear to have been a problem but the Dutch example shows that reliance on continued house price inflation is a risky long term policy for any social housing scheme.

▶ **Political constraints** have been most clearly a problem in the case of the Hessen Foundation. Soon after our research was completed the Red/Green government in Hessen unexpectedly collapsed. The new Christian Democratic administration cut off the Foundation's funding. Despite the attempt to set up the Foundation so it would be immune to political attack, this was not to be. Ironically, this was because, as a publicly funded body, the previous government had felt obliged to retain certain controls over how the foundation operated and a strong representation on its governing bodies. With the benefit of hindsight, it is all too apparent that it is very difficult to combine financial dependence with political independence.

▶ **Legal problems** have often accompanied the new forms of social housing. Various projects are attempting to combine the best features of social renting and owner occupation; to provide occupants with a stake in their housing; to democratise management; and to ensure long term availability for lower-income households. The use of land leases with special 'social use' clauses have proved an important way of securing social housing run by private owners.

In this context, private ownership has a range of meanings. In the case of socially bound ownership it involves individual owners, while in the case of the Hessen Foundation it involves various forms of collectives, co-operatives and associations.

However, especially in Germany and the Netherlands, current legislation inhibits the forming of such bodies. The general view is that there are enough suitable existing organisations which can accommodate new initiatives. Some argue, though, for the formation of new, smaller collective organisations which allow for self-management and greater accountability, rejecting the undemocratic nature of most existing larger scale social housing institutions. And in Germany many new small-scale co-operatives are being attempted in the face of opposition from the established social housing federal bodies and lengthy and difficult legal procedures.

Most of these projects arose as a result of initiatives taken 'from below' rather than policies imposed 'from above'. This is radically different from the way in which post-war social housing has developed. It is, in some respects, a return to the pattern of such housing earlier in the century when groups of workers formed housing co-operatives. Much of this activism was lost when social housing became a major welfare state programme after 1945. As a result a great deal of the early popular commitment to the tenure was dissipated. This loss has contributed to the contemporary problems of managing such housing and to its declining political fortunes by removing any sense that its occupants have a stake in their housing and its long term maintenance.

Many of the projects also involve attempts to develop new forms of social housing that are meeting particular needs which social housing has largely ignored in the past. The two most radically innovatory projects in this respect are the Rotterdam scheme which involves a form of 'social owner-occupation' and the Purmerend project which houses those who wish to maintain communal patterns of living. Many of the projects also show the need for organisations which will provide technical assistance and advice as well as some funding, or access to funding, to groups of lower-income households who wish to establish new forms of social housing. The existing arrangements for the production of social housing are, in most cases, ill-adapted to encompass these new developments and the necessity for new 'enabling' organisations is evident.

To summarise, these projects involve markedly different ways of providing a permanent supply of affordable social housing from those which have been customary. All the projects are trying to provide housing well suited to the particular needs and incomes of their occupants. All of them place great emphasis on shifting the principal responsibility for their design, management and overall control away from 'external' and centralised organisations towards the occupants, whether as individuals or on a collective basis (or normally some combination of these two).

It is interesting to contrast this approach with current British policies for the break-up of the existing system of social housing provision. On the whole, this is a much less radical reform than the new developments we have reviewed here. Although there is some reference to council housing being transferred to its tenants, there is as yet no real evidence that this will become a major development.

Most council housing is likely to be transferred to new bodies such as Housing Action Trusts or other landlords such as housing associations or the private sector, thus preserving the type of relationship between tenants and landlords which has typified both sectors of rental housing. It remains to be seen whether such changes of ownership will make any real difference to the various problems of the social housing sector, which some have seen simply as a product of public ownership. In contrast, the projects reviewed in this chapter do contribute to the search for new forms of social housing. They involve a more radical break with its recent history and may offer more than the types of change now being initiated in Britain to ensure that the recent decline of this major source of affordable housing is reversed.

3. New Management Structures in Social Housing

In the previous chapter we examined several innovatory forms of social housing provision, most of which involve a degree of resident responsibility for management. There has been much discussion of decentralised management operating within existing forms of social housing in Britain and abroad. The most common and most limited form of devolution involves the decentralisation of traditional, centrally controlled management structures to local estates, plus, perhaps, increased tenant consultation and participation. The further step of transferring the principal management responsibilities to the tenants is, as yet, relatively rare, although the example of the Glasgow co-operatives has, of course, received much publicity.

Discussion about decentralised management has been stimulated by the attempts of many governments and social housing landlords to manage 'problem' or 'hard to let' estates. By bringing management nearer to the tenants and involving them to a greater degree, and by providing resources for the physical upgrading of the housing and its environment, it is hoped the decline of these areas can be halted and their financial and social problems resolved. Apart from this special situation which, even today, only applies to a very limited amount of social housing, there is the more general critique of centralised and unresponsive management (to which we have already referred in earlier chapters). So decentralisation and tenant participation is seen as having a potential for application throughout the social housing stock.

In our research we visited several projects located on problem ridden social housing estates (for example, the Bijlmermeer estate near Amsterdam and the Märkische Viertel project in Berlin). The innovatory policies being developed on such estates are very similar to those which were pioneered in Britain by the Priority Estates Project. So we have chosen in this chapter to concentrate on two examples of tenant management schemes. These illustrate some of the key opportunities and problems which this approach entails. One of the projects is a response to the problems of severely deteriorated public housing in the United States. The other involves a newly built social housing estate in Amsterdam.

Tenant management in Jersey City

From the mid-seventies onwards, there have been widely publicised experiments in tenant management in a few American public housing projects. Much experience has been obtained about the conditions under which tenant management can operate effectively. This is why it was important to examine one of these projects in our research.

Tenant management began in St Louis after a series of dramatic events in the early 1970s, including the demolition of the Pruitt Igoe housing complex barely 15 years after it had been built, an action which became a symbol of the seemingly insoluble problems of US public housing. This was accompanied by a rent strike among tenants of the St Louis Housing Authority and its subsequent bankruptcy.

The development of tenant management was, at first, a crisis response. If the tenants had not taken over their projects the housing authority would have collapsed and they would probably have lost their homes. As the first tenant management project in US public housing, St Louis got extensive media and political attention and obtained large-scale financial support from the Ford Foundation and other sources. This experience led, later in the 1970s, to a national demonstration programme funded by the federal government. The Jersey City Housing Authority was a participant in this programme.

Public housing began in the USA in the 1930s. It was never intended as a major alternative to private rental housing but as a limited programme to house some of the 'submerged middle class', formerly well paid workers who had lost their jobs and housing in the Depression. Public house building was also a means of combating unemployment in the building industry.

After 1949, when such roles were no longer relevant, it became closely linked to urban renewal programmes, housing low-income, especially black, households displaced from clearance areas. Public housing also accommodated some of the low-income elderly. Access was restricted to those on very low incomes – roughly in the bottom quarter of the income distribution. By the 1970s public housing accommodated, often on separate estates, high concentrations of white, elderly, low-income households and of black, single parent families. Most tenants were dependent on welfare benefits.

Public housing was originally subsidised by federal government contributions which met the capital costs. The running costs were met out of rental income. By the 1960s this arrangement was breaking down. There was an increasing concentration of very low-income tenants with limited ability to pay, on the one hand, and rapid increases in operating costs, caused by inflation, on the other. Public housing authorities could only raise rents to levels which imposed an impossible burden on their tenants or cut back drastically on management and maintenance and watch the projects deteriorate. In practice, they did both.

However, in 1969 Congress decided that tenants should not pay more than 25 per cent of 'adjusted income' in rent. This meant that the government had to provide additional operating subsidies. These rapidly escalated over the next decade.

Public housing has been constantly under political attack. This has resulted in its being run according to rules which have contributed greatly to its problems. By the 1960s it had lost its earlier reputation for providing decent and affordable housing and was increasingly unpopular. Public housing tenants were stigmatised and governments which wanted to support lower-income housing looked to other methods. Yet, the poor reputation of public housing and its tenants was the product of conditions in some of the larger housing projects in the big cities. In many smaller towns, which had smaller projects, it continued to be a useful and, on the whole, well regarded form of low-income housing.

Despite the new subsidies, the condition of public housing in many of the large urban centres continued to deteriorate in the 1970s. A contributory cause was remote, bureaucratic and even authoritarian management. In addition, many projects had been built to very low standards, in high density blocks with few or no communal facilities, little landscaping and so on. This was because Congress was determined to ensure that public housing was as 'economically' provided as possible (and the private property lobby wanted to ensure that it could not be a competitor). So there was a need for very large-scale investment to repair and improve public housing. Congress eventually provided some subsidies but the approach to modernisation, and the arrangements for distributing operating subsidies, have been ill thought out and have not enabled most troubled public housing authorities to solve their difficulties.

The Jersey City Housing Authority is one such example. It owns about 4,000 apartments on nine sites, one for elderly people and eight for families. By the early 1980s, 75 per cent of the tenants were black, nine per cent Hispanic and 16 per cent white. Nearly three quarters of the households had welfare payments as their main source of income. By the early 1970s, six of the projects were, in the words of its current director, Robert Rigby, 'in an abominable condition' with inoperable utility systems, structural faults, massive vandalism, piles of rubbish around the sites and a high rate of vacancies and rent arrears. Crime was also a severe problem on these as on many other such housing projects.

At the same time, the authority was enmeshed in a corrupt system of city politics and its management practices were, at best, incompetent and, at worst, corrupt. In fact, any semblance of accountable management had disappeared and the authority was on the verge of bankruptcy.

This began to change in 1973 when a new reform mayor took office, new housing authority commissioners were installed and new staff hired, including Robert Rigby as director. The authority urgently needed to start rescuing its severely deteriorated housing projects but it was virtually bankrupt and there was no possibility of getting extra finance from the federal government. It was forced to begin work on just one site and try to persuade the tenants to help provide the management input which it could not afford to supply. This was how tenant management emerged in Jersey City, as a rather desperate response to an acute crisis.

The tenants were used to poor and unresponsive management which ignored their protests about conditions. So it was not easy to win their co-operation. According to the director, it was necessary to show that tenant involvement would be in their interest, to generate tenant self-confidence through the organising process and to link tenant rights and responsibilities.

Rigby describes the project, 'A. Harry Moore', and its conditions in 1973 as, '*a family complex of seven, 12-storey, brick buildings laid out in an oval pattern on three hectares and comprised of 662 units of one to four bedrooms, "vintage" fifties architecture, driven by land economics, dominated by a-number-of-units-produced mentality...with long-term durability and livability being afterthoughts....By 1973, estate conditions were abysmal. On ten of the sites, 14 urine-stenched elevators were inoperable and had been for almost half a year. Deteriorated utility systems resulted in chronically erratic services. Public spaces, such as hallways, stairwells and building lobbies lay vandalised and debris-ridden; an engulfing state of squalor. Approximately 20 per cent of project apartments had been permanently abandoned, with vacancies increasing at a rate of almost 15 a month. Crime and vandalism were the behavioral norm; fear and hopelessness the pervasive ethos*'.

Eighty five per cent of its residents belonged to ethnic minorities, most were black; 68 per cent were single parent households; most gained their main income from welfare benefits. In short, it was a hard case to start on.

However, a small group of tenants wished to co-operate with the new housing authority. This provided the nucleus for the new tenant organisation. After long negotiations the tenants and the authority began to work with what Rigby describes as '*...an odd blend of scepticism, desperation and hope*'. The authority agreed to use some of its very limited resources to rehabilitate the interior public space of one of the seven buildings. In exchange, the tenants organised a lobby patrol to monitor access to the building in the evenings, when most vandalism and crime occurred, and to ensure that the improvements were not wrecked. Rehabilitating the public spaces involved minor repairs and redecoration and was relatively cheap but it greatly improved the appearance of the block. It also established a process in which, in exchange for tenant involvement in the project, the authority improved conditions.

The tenants group then began to enlist the support of other tenants in the building. The promise of improvement in exchange for participation was a key reason why this succeeded. Soon other buildings wished to join in the process and a distinctive tenant organisation and tenant leaders began to emerge. Eventually the authority's slim resources began to run out. The new tenant organisation began to protest that the housing authority was failing to meet its side of the bargain. At this point, the authority was rescued by support from the state government, which gave funding for staff to develop tenant organisation and for rehabilitation.

As the building improved, there was some increase in applications for the vacant units which were a financial liability and a source of continued dereliction. Some funds were used to make these habitable and in 18 months the vacancy rate fell from 19 per cent to eight per cent. The reduction in vacant units also helped to improve site security and the crime rate fell dramatically. Vandalism was also notably reduced throughout the project. This was probably due not just to the tenant lobby patrols but also to a general improvement in the whole atmosphere and ethos surrounding the project. This change was aided by the social and other activities which began to develop around the tenant organisation.

After three years the tenant organisation was well established. However, the housing authority still controlled most aspects of management and there had not been much improvement in management quality. As Rigby notes, despite some improvements in its administration, the authority remained a 'nine-to-five owner' and its management performance at the estate level 'remained marginal, continued to reflect its absentee status and was a persisting source of tenant frustration'.

The authority was aware of the pioneering development of tenant management in St Louis but was ambivalent about whether it wanted to initiate this in its own stock. But in 1976 the federal government announced a national tenant management demonstration programme co-sponsored by the Ford Foundation. The Jersey City project was invited to join the programme and its tenant leaders were eager to accept because of their dissatisfaction with the authority's management.

The project was one of six in the national programme. Its tenant management was to be structured along the lines of the St Louis project. This involved setting up a private non-profit tenant management corporation with an elected non-paid resident Board of Directors. The Board would be trained over a nine to twelve month period in all aspects of management. It would then, in consultation with all the tenants, develop a set of rules for the running of the project, taking account of existing federal and local regulations.

The tenant management corporation would hire its own paid management staff from among the.project residents. Site maintenance personnel would remain employed by the authority but would be supervised by the tenant managers. After the staff were trained, over a further period of nine to fifteen months, the management corporation would take over the project. The authority would continue to be responsible for centralised services such as purchasing, insurance, extraordinary maintenance, payroll processing and technical assistance, its costs being charged to the management corporation. It would also retain ownership of the project and remain accountable for it to the federal government.

The whole process of establishing a tenant management corporation, hiring staff and training took from summer 1976 to autumn 1978. The tenant managers developed what the authority director described as a 'conservative' set of project rules. These made it clear that failure to observe lease terms, control childrens' behaviour, pay rent on time or assist in cleaning the common parts of the building would rapidly lead to eviction. Also, the managers intended to run a restrictive admissions policy. In short, tenant management would be far less 'liberal' than the previous regime.

All the paid staff employed by the management corporation had to be site residents and the manager appointed in each building had to live there. The training sessions were run by two experienced consultants who had advised the St Louis tenants. It was intensive and time consuming for the tenant managers and the authority staff. One advantage of tenant management was that the corporation staff had a far greater knowledge of the circumstances of individual tenants than the remote authority staff. However, this closeness also meant that tenant managers were under severe pressure when they had to take some form of drastic action, such as eviction.

By the late 1970s the project was under tenant management and there had been striking improvements in the condition of the buildings. The vacancy rate had fallen below two per cent, the repairs backlog had fallen to a very low level and the number of households over a month in rent arrears had fallen from more than a fifth to below a tenth. The management corporation had attracted a somewhat wider income mix of tenants than hitherto and the average rent obtained from each unit had risen by over a quarter.

Meanwhile a similar effort had been underway at a second project, Curries Woods. A grim looking complex of seven 12 and 13 storey, reinforced concrete and brick buildings, it contained 712 apartments and was first occupied in 1959. By the 1970s it was in much the same state as A. Harry Moore had been. However, despite also being included in the national demonstration project, this was dogged by antagonistic relations between the tenants and the authority. Little progress was made and there was a constant turnover of the tenant leadership. By the late seventies the attempt to establish tenant management had to be abandoned. The project reverted to conventional management and its deterioration continued into the 1980s.

Tenants also began organising at a third site – Montgomery Gardens – in the mid-seventies. This is very similar to A. Harry Moore but has 462 apartments in six 10-storey blocks. The major difference is that, unlike Harry Moore, Montgomery Gardens has no hallway or stairwell windows – 'a particularly crass example of architectural innovation', according to Robert Rigby.

The tenants pressed the housing authority – which was reluctant to move too fast – to agree to the establishment of a tenant management corporation ('We're ready! The tenants have been ready! What the hell are you people waiting for, Christmas? It'll come and go twice, at the rate you're going!'). This was not included in the national demonstration project and received fewer resources to set it up. But by late 1979, after a two year period of preparation, tenant management took over with results that were as satisfactory as those of the first project.

At the time of our research, the two sites were still under tenant management. The improvements in their condition and finances had been maintained. A third site had recently converted to tenant management. On all three sites there had been major investments in improving the housing and environment. The internal public spaces are clean, well lit and decorated. The basic services functioned properly. As much as possible of the surrounding grounds are split up into separate plots, all entrances were given their own courtyards, with a choice of arrangements between fencing, flower pots and walkways. Low fences indicate 'private space' for which individual tenants are responsible. Areas are designated for specific activities, like a basketball court and playgrounds for younger children decentralised around the site.

All this has made a vital contribution to ensuring the success of tenant management. As Rigby notes, 'If a parent needed to wrap three blankets round each of her children to ward off the cold and keep them out of the room where the roof is leaking, it would not have been reasonable to expect any receptivity to "getting involved".' In fact, the housing authority was unwilling to support tenant management unless it could also be sure that major funding for physical works would be available. The cost of this work averaged $20,000 per unit.

Each tenant management corporation has an annual budget. The federal operating subsidies are allocated to public housing authorities by a formula which purports to estimate what is required to maintain a reasonably well run housing authority, deducts estimated rental income, allowing for low levels of vacancies and arrears, and covers the gap between the two figures. There is intense argument about whether the formula is adequate, especially for hard pressed urban authorities such as the Jersey City one. Modernisation subsidies are allocated on an extremely unsatisfactory ad hoc basis.

The housing authority divides its operating subsidy among the individual projects, most of which are still conventionally managed. About two fifths of the project budget is spent on utilities (which are included in the rent). The tenant managers have no control over this. There are other items which also cannot be controlled by the tenants such as insurance and union-agreed employee benefits.

So the discretionary element in the budget is small. It includes items such as security protection and tenant services, such as recreation programmes. The tenants have some control over maintenance staff but all skilled workers are employed by the authority. The allocation of new tenancies is controlled to a considerable degree by a mass of federal rules and regulations but on the tenant managed sites potentially eligible applicants are interviewed by the tenant managers and rejected if they are not acceptable.

On three of the authority's sites, tenants had decided not to take over the management. They felt that this was the authority's responsibility. Interestingly, on these sites the conditions under conventional management were considerably better than they had been on the sites currently managed by tenants before the tenants took over. In one case – which we visited – this was because the authority had spent a great deal on improvement, averaging $55,000 per unit.

Unlike the 1970s, there has recently been a considerable demand for public housing. In 1987 the housing authority had a waiting list of 6,000 and only a five per cent annual turnover of units. However, the changed situation is probably as much a result of the growth of unemployment and rapidly escalating private sector rents as of the changes which have occurred in public housing management.

The Half World housing project – Amsterdam

The Half World housing project in Amsterdam gets its name from a Dutch saying which refers to people who will gain half the world by being ambitious. It provides a radically contrasting example of tenant management. Half World is a recently built development which has been under tenant management from the beginning. Moreover, here tenant management is not a response to crisis conditions but a much more considered attempt to break away from old style, centralised and bureaucratic but still reasonably functional, housing management.

The project consists of 120 units housing 250 people. It contains a wide range of differently sized units, the largest having seven rooms and the smallest being one room plus kitchen. It is a low rise development designed to fit into the historic neighbourhood in which it is located – with a large and attractive garden.

Amsterdam city council's housing company has a stock of about 30,000 public housing units. Up to the early 1980s housing management was centralised but divided on a functional basis into semi-autonomous bureaucratic fiefdoms. According to Felix van der Laar, an ex-official of the housing company who had worked with the tenants in establishing tenant management, in the late 1970s there was a conflict within the housing company between the old guard and younger managers, who were critical of the department's performance. These reformers were supported by tenants' organisations.

Eventually, the authority was reorganised on a more decentralised basis with seven area offices. The headquarters' functions were limited to major policy making, co-ordination and handling relations with local politicians. The new managers also wanted to develop tenant participation. They set up a framework for electing tenant councils at estate, area and central levels. However, this is a 'top down', rather bureaucratic model which is not very effective in practice. Few tenants participate in the elections or on the councils. They prefer to develop their own grassroots organisations.

This was the general background to Half World but the project was also a response to the specific history of the area in which it is located. This is the Nieuwmarkt, one of the oldest areas of the city with many fine buildings. In the 1960s and 1970s there was intense local protest as the new underground railway came through the area and many buildings were demolished. Half World is located on a part of the cleared area.

The site had been owned by the Union of Dutch Architects which wanted to redevelop it commercially, although it had formerly been a residential area. The Union was put under great pressure by a local group and by socially committed architects. So it sold the site to the city for housing. The question then was whether it should be developed by a housing association or by the city. The community group which had led the protest against commercial redevelopment had been thinking about what sort of housing scheme should be built. A housing association which had been willing to take the site on, faced with this grassroots involvement, withdrew as it did not want to share design and management responsibilities with others. So the municipal housing company took over the redevelopment.

The company consulted the community group about the design of the project (the group contained several architects and other professionals). While the building went ahead, the department and the local group also discussed how the project would be run and a scheme for tenant management emerged.

Eventually a very detailed agreement was worked out between the local authority and the tenants. Van der Laar told us, '...the main principle is to let the tenants do as much as possible and minimise the housing company's role'. The tenant organisation has most of the responsibility for running the project and budgeting, while the local authority retains the overall responsibility to central government for the accounts and for ensuring that the subsidy rules are followed. Rents are set by national legislation and the subsidies are similarly determined. The tenants are allowed a two per cent deduction from the required rent income for voids and arrears.

There is an elected board of tenant managers and many activities, such as rent collecting and maintaining the garden, are done on a voluntary basis. However, some staff are hired for maintenance and book-keeping. These posts are funded out of a fixed allowance which the tenants receive from the rent and subsidy income. This has to cover maintenance, administration, property taxes, insurance and other running costs. The formula which determines this allowance is set nationally: the housing company keeps one tenth towards its own costs (less than the real cost) and passes the rest on to the tenants.

The housing company tries to be involved as little as possible in the day to day running of the estate. It has no formal presence on the elected tenant council although there are frequent informal consultations between the tenants and the housing officials involved in the project. The housing company retains the ownership of the project and has to inspect the accounts annually. The tenant board consists of nine people. It meets daily but there is also an executive which consists of the president, secretary and treasurer. The board has various subcommittees which involve another ten or so tenants, dealing with maintenance, gardening, book-keeping and rent collecting. The original plan was to have general meetings of tenants three times a year – in fact, this only occurs annually when the board is elected.

There has been no great competition for places on the board and when the first president retired there had only been one candidate to replace him. Tenant management is very time consuming yet it is not retired people who most often get involved but those in their 30s and 40s who are already very active in other matters. People tend to become heavily involved for a time then drop out as other commitments accumulate, they get 'burnt out', or reach a stage in child rearing which is very time consuming.

Half of the project housing was initially allocated to households that had answered advertisements in the area. The other half went to households displaced by urban renewal elsewhere in the city. Both groups knew that they would be entering a tenant managed scheme and the urban renewal tenants could have chosen to be allocated units elsewhere. It could, therefore, be assumed that some initial level of commitment to self-manage-ment existed, although the site was in a very good central location. So some tenants undoubtedly chose to live there for this reason.

The tenants have a wide range of occupations and incomes. However, there is no income limit on eligibility. This results in a high concentration of well educated, younger (20 to 40 year old) tenants in professional occupa-tions. According to Felix van der Laar, ' *the tenants are the most highly educated group of tenants in municipal housing. Many are yuppies and there is even one university professor*'. Many of them are socially aware and politically active but, especially as a result of the allocation from urban renewal areas, there are also a considerable number of older and lower-income tenants and some ethnic minority households.

Despite the rather limited level of participation, tenants generally feel that their elected management is closer to them and more responsive to their problems than old-style management would be. The board members have a contact hour on Saturdays when anyone with problems can see them and maintenance committee members can be contacted at any time if there are problems.

According to van der Laar, '*tenants tend to divide into the "respectable" who are concerned to keep the project clean and well maintained and "hippy types" who have a more free and easy approach*'. This creates some tensions which the board has tried to resolve. At the time of the research it had only evicted one tenant, for non-payment of rent. The garden is an important source of tenant involvement. They have invested a good deal of their own resources in it, for plants, play equipment and other facilities. Many tenants voluntarily help to maintain it.

However, about one third of the tenants make no contribution to running the project. The tenant board is unhappy about this and about people who have complaints but make no positive contribution. But this does not seem to be an acute source of tension so far.

Vacancies are allocated according to the procedure that the city used in the private rental sector which is less strict than that used in social housing (in the Netherlands housing stress areas, such as Amsterdam, have controls over who is allocated most vacant housing, including private rented and owner-occupied units up to a certain rent or price level). This means that the tenants can fill vacancies provided that applicants meet the general council rules controlling access to housing (these relate to length of previous residence in the city or the possession of a job there).

This system applies to half the vacancies, for the other half these residence/job rules are much less restrictive. A subcommittee of the board together with some co-opted tenants make the choice; they have a long waiting list. Given its location, if the project was conventionally managed there would be a strong demand for it but tenant management ensures that vacancies are filled far faster than would occur under normal management. There has not yet been enough experience of tenant allocation to say whether this is more conservative than allocation by the department.

But the experience of an eviction made the tenants very careful in their assessment of applicants, as rent arrears have serious consequences for project finances. Prospective tenants are informally interviewed before being admitted to the waiting list. They are then housed in order of date and degree of need (for example, when a vacancy occurs they may consider the top ten on the list who are eligible, given the size of the unit, and choose one according to the degree of need). So far there is no evidence of discrimination on race or other grounds.

A big problem is the lack of tenant expertise. Unlike the Jersey City tenants they have no special training. They find it difficult to manage matters such as repair and maintenance work. In addition, because of the small size of the project, they are in a rather weak position when negotiating terms with contractors and they obtain less good prices for work than the local authority. The other big question is whether there will always be enough active tenants prepared to take over the management.

There is a division between those tenants who take a more pragmatic stance and those who stick to certain principles come what may. This conflict had been highlighted by a plan which involved the loss of some of the project garden to another development (this had been an agreed condition for the housing development going ahead initially). Some tenants wanted to compromise and others to resist the development totally. The board wanted to compromise but was outvoted at a tenants' meeting and so tenant managers felt they could not continue negotiating with the council over the problem. At the time of our research this problem remained unresolved.

Van der Laar believes that the local authority's traditional housing managers are rather sceptical about the development, especially concerning whether it can be sustained by the tenants. It will take perhaps five to ten years to see whether the scheme will perform effectively and survive. Unlike the Jersey City projects the decision to set up Half World had been made deliberately by the new management which had taken over the department because of its belief in decentralisation and tenant participation.

It had not resulted from financial pressures; indeed these managers were extremely hesitant about giving the tenants as much financial responsibility as they eventually obtained. According to van der Laar, they had been worried that the tenants might 'run off to the Bermudas with the money'. But he had argued, successfully, that budgetary control by the tenants was essential if the idea was to be seriously tried out. In practice, the tenants have been very responsible in their handling of money.

Another tricky issue for the local authority department is to maintain its policy of not intervening in the day to day affairs of the tenant management and allowing it to make its own mistakes, thus learning by them. One factor which has generally helped the tenants in their negotiations with officials is that the project has been supported by the government's Experimental Housing Foundation (see chapter seven). As already noted, officials do not attend board meetings but they do get board minutes and are informally consulted. So far the scheme is rather an isolated experiment. There is no strong feeling among the councillors that it should be extended to other social housing estates. Nor are the local housing associations taking up the idea. But there have been many visitors to the scheme from other cities and similar projects are underway in Rotterdam and the Hague.

Discussion

Jersey City Housing Authority and Half World developed their tenant management schemes under very different circumstances. In Jersey City tenants took over for wholly pragmatic reasons and in circumstances of extreme crisis for the existing housing management. In Half World tenant management was a far more deliberate experiment promoted by managers and a community based organisation responding to a general dissatisfaction with centralised management rather than to any immediate crisis.

The Jersey City tenants have very low incomes and most lack much in the way of formal educational qualifications. The Half World tenants have a much wider income and social mix with a strong representation of professionals and others who are ideologically committed to self-management. The Jersey City projects are located in old and deteriorating buildings with many problems such as a high crime rate, vandalism, high vacancies and so on. Half World is a new and attractive project with none of these problems. The American tenant management corporations were only established after a long process of building tenant organisation from grassroots and training residents. The tenant management arrangements for Half World were worked out before the tenants moved in and they had to learn 'on the job'.

In both cases, tenant management seems to be working. But both are, in some senses, special cases and not typical of normal social housing estates in either country. The socio-economic composition of the Half World tenants is unusually biased towards the better off and more educated. In Amsterdam, at least, there seems to be a significant proportion of such people who have a high degree of principled commitment to tenant management. Such people also have many of the general skills with which to carry it out. In Jersey City not only were conditions extreme, even by the standards of US public housing, but these also provide a strong reason why tenants are prepared to organise and get involved.

Present indications are that tenant management is not likely to develop on a major scale. We have already referred to the limited impact which Half World has had elsewhere in Amsterdam and in the Netherlands and noted that tenants in some of the other Jersey City projects decided against self-management or were unable to carry it through. At the time of our research there had been little addition to the numbers of tenant-managed US public housing projects which had existed at the time of the national demonstration programme in the 1970s. This amounted to less than a dozen sites in all.

The experience of these two projects suggests that there are several reasons why tenant management may have limited application. Or, to put it another way, they indicate the prerequisites of its success. The initial requirement is motivation. Why should tenants take over? As we saw in New Jersey, this was essentially because it was in their self- interest to do so and in Half World because of a principled commitment to tenant management (plus some people saw it as a way of obtaining desirable housing!).

However, as the responses from some of the less deteriorated Jersey City projects showed, many tenants believe that management should be a professional service supplied in exchange for rent payments, not something which they should be expected to carry out. Interestingly, Felix van der Laar told us that he had recently been asked to go and talk to some working class tenants of a social housing estate in Eindhoven. The tenants had been struggling, without success, to get repairs done and were now considering whether to take over the estate management. However, 'they wanted to have control but not be responsible for all the business...this was what most people were likely to want. They don't have the time or the inclination to replace paid management. They want to get the bureaucracy to take up and deal with their problems. At the moment they tend to get fobbed off by the bureaucracy which shelters behind politicians in refusing to do anything until or unless the problem becomes large scale'.

The issue of motivation leads to a second consideration, the question of the resources of time and skills available to the tenants. Tenant management is very time consuming and many tenants do not have the time available, especially when they are tied to the daily routine of full-time, paid employment away from the projects. We have already referred to what almost appeared to be a life cycle of involvement in the management of Half World, with people becoming active and then dropping out as their circumstances changed. In Jersey City there is a high proportion of households with no paid employment, especially many woman headed single parent families. The demands of bringing up a family single-handed are very great and yet these women have taken the lead in establishing and staffing the tenant management corporations.

The skills required for tenant management are extensive, far greater than those required of the individual owner-occupier, for example. Half World manages because it is small scale, a new project with few real problems, as yet, and because many of its residents have a high level of general education, are articulate and are politically and socially involved. The Jersey City tenants are poor and lack this educational background and are also tackling very difficult problems. For all these reasons there had to be a lengthy and quite costly period of training before they could take over.

There are several fears which professional housing managers often voice at the idea of tenant management. These include the costs and whether tenant managers will handle financial matters responsibly. On these counts, as well as their efficiency over rent arrears and voids, Jersey City and Half World perform at least as well as traditional management and sometimes better.

Another fear concerns allocation and the enforcement of tenancy rules. In neither case is there any evidence of discrimination or an inability to take hard decisions over tenancy matters. In fact, the Jersey City tenant managers are more conservative in their practices in respect to, for example, pre-admission screening, than conventional management. Given their situation, this is wholly understandable but it does raise difficult issues concerning the role which social housing plays in accommodating families with social, financial or other problems.

In a series of publications, Robert Rigby, the Jersey City Housing Authority director has drawn together the main lessons which have been learnt from his experience of tenant management. He has managed to isolate some of the key conditions, in addition to those discussed above, which are required for the tenant management corporations to work successfully. These are:-

▶ Decentralising and reorganising management services, especially maintenance, which remain under the control of the housing authority. This includes estate-based managers controlling the maintenance staff and establishing and monitoring performance standards throughout the authority.

▶ A lengthy and intensive period of building up a relationship with the tenants, in which both management and tenants agree to make contributions to improving the projects. Tenant management has to be seen by tenants as something which will directly benefit them before they will become involved.

▶ The emergence of a stable tenant leadership on the projects. The successful Jersey City schemes all had this, the one that failed did not. There was a rapid rate of turnover of tenancies at the failed project; tenant management works best where there is, at least, a core of long term, stable households.

▶ A management corporation structure worked out with the tenants which draws on their grassroots forms of organisation rather than a model which is imposed 'top down'.

▶ Finally, apart from tenants needing extensive training, the authority's own staff also need training and professional help, as they are required to work in new and unaccustomed ways with tenants.

4. New Ways of Funding Lower-Income Housing

The British government has recently emphasised policies which aim to increase the direct involvement of the private sector in the regeneration of urban areas, starting with the establishment of the first Urban Development Corporations and Enterprise Zones in the early 1980s. Some housing associations and local authorities have obtained private sector loans to sustain housing investment at a time when public funding has been drastically reduced. Schemes for mixed housing association funding and limited investor tax subsidies have been two consequences of this general trend towards private sector funding. The 1988 Housing Act, which establishes Housing Action Trusts and aims to revive private rented housing, is predicated on an, as yet, untested belief that very substantial direct private investment can be obtained.

In this chapter we examine innovative ways of bringing private capital to low-income housing. Some schemes involve partnerships between local government, the private sector and locally-based housing development. In Britain, the Netherlands and Germany, one consequence of declining central government support for lower-income housing has been to transfer greater responsibility for meeting housing needs to local government. However, as government resources have been reduced, localities are under pressure to develop new ways of responding to housing needs. This is resulting in a variety of new policies. For example, in Germany and the Netherlands some local authorities have tried to use regulatory powers to control rent levels and to preserve access to lower-income housing. Often such initiatives are, hardly surprisingly, strongly opposed by private sector property interests and by central government.

Another strategy is to develop closer forms of collaboration including formal partnership agreements. In Britain the 1988 Housing Act envisages fundamental changes in the role of local housing authorities, including a new role in relation to the private sector and locally-based but independent landlords, tenant co-operatives and so on. Essentially, the local authorities have been told to use their limited resources to help promote increased activity by others to meet housing needs. This new form of partnership between public, private and community-based organisations has already emerged in many American cities.

In this chapter we examine some of these schemes as well as two organisations which promote them – the Local Initiatives Support Corporation and the Enterprise Foundation. Our focus is on American projects because, as we discovered in the research, the most interesting developments so far have occurred there. We first sketch in the general background to these schemes, then discuss them. Finally, we consider a range of other projects, starting with some Chicago-based schemes which have had a significant impact in that city and on developments elsewhere.

General background

Urban decline and renewal: The decline of US inner city areas which sparked off the widespread riots of the 1960s continued and spread in succeeding years. In many cities the de-industrialization of the past decade has also resulted in many formerly stable working class neighbourhoods beyond the urban core being blighted. Many of these areas have high concentrations of rented property whose profitability has declined as local incomes have stagnated and costs have continued to rise. Landlord disinvestment and ultimately the abandonment of their property has often occurred. At the same time, in some cities new employment in the service sector has increased. Typically, this generates a polarised economic structure, with relatively few high paying jobs and a larger number of low paid jobs. This polarisation is reflected in the housing market, where some areas of potentially attractive housing are being gentrified and their former lower-income residents displaced, but other much larger areas continue to decline.

Reductions in federal assistance: In the 1960s there was a substantial increase in federal assistance for inner city areas, including subsidised housing programmes which, while inadequate in relation to the scale of needs, were on a large scale compared to what had occurred before or since. From the early seventies these programmes were cut back and since 1981 the federal government has tried to end its commitment to new subsidised low-income housing.

By the mid-eighties all that remained, apart from a few units still in the building pipeline, were some limited subsidies for lower-income housing rehabilitation and a small programme of 'housing vouchers' – payments which were intended to allow lower-income households to obtain affordable private rented housing. Very few of these were available in each locality and many eligible households were unable to find accommodation which was of an acceptable standard for inclusion in the programme. Ethnic minority households had particular difficulties due to widespread discrimination in letting.

Other sources of assistance: Since the 1960s tax shelters had been available for some lower-income housing development and rehabilitation. These enabled 'high net worth' individuals to invest, as limited partners, in rental housing and obtain depreciation allowances which could be used to shelter other income. Following a major federal tax reform in 1986 these schemes were replaced by tax credits which encouraged corporate rather than personal investment in low-income housing. The programme is due to run for three years, from 1987 to 1990. The amount of tax credit available is limited on a state by state basis, control over the use of the credits resting with state governments.

In addition, some states support low-income housing. In particular, they issue tax-free bonds to support housing development. These only provide slightly cheaper capital, have often been used to support middle rather than low-income housing and have now also been limited by federal legislation. Finally, some cities provide assistance, although the dire state of local government finance in many declining urban areas makes this difficult. However, the general Community Development Block Grant, provided on a formula basis by the federal government, is used by localities for a wide variety of programmes which are supposed to be targeted on declining neighbourhoods. Some of these funds are used for housing. In addition, many cities grant property tax relief for new housing development, including low-income housing.

Community-based activism: Many American cities have an extensive net-work of community-based organisations which carry out an enormous range of activities. Some arose out of the community protests of the 1960s, many are backed by churches, local business organisations, local charities and so on. Some have highly professional paid staff, others run on a voluntary basis. Some are highly democratic, others less so – although most have local residents on their boards of directors. Many of these groups are based in neighbourhoods which have been faced with disinvestment and decline and are committed to reversing this process. The rehabilitation and development of new housing has been a major objective of many such 'community development corporations', along with local economic development.

In the past decade many big cities have seen the emergence of specialist 'neighbourhood housing developers' and organisations established to serv-ice and press for resources for such developers. Up to the 1980s many of these developers were crucially dependent on federal subsidies to lower the costs of housing which they provided, so bringing it within the range of lower-income households. Since the withdrawal of federal subsidies the neighbourhood housing developers have had to look for other resources, from city and state governments and from the private sector.

Corporate and charitable involvement : Corporate and charitable activity has had a significant impact in some inner city areas. Most corporate decision making has had negative consequences for such areas (plant closures, urban renewal and displacement). As a reporter on the Chicago Sun-Times put it, in relation to that city, *'Chicago is that toddlin' town where corporate brass grabs the 4.45 commuter train and then looks the other way while gliding past rundown city neighborhoods'*. However, he went on to note that, *'a startling new breeze is blowing now'*.

What he was referring to, in this city and elsewhere, is that support has been growing for neighbourhood reinvestment. Apart from any policy of demonstrating 'good citizenship', this is often for sound business reasons. For example, some companies wish to stem decline in the cities where their headquarters are located and some financial institutions are acting to protect local investments. Corporate support for charitable endeavour is, anyway, a long established US tradition and local community groups have exerted legal or political pressure for such support. A few major national charities (notably the Ford Foundation) have been heavily committed to supporting innovative community-based developments since the 1960s. We will now discuss one of the major Ford Foundation initiatives which seeks to channel private capital into low-income housing.

The Local Initiatives Support Corporation

The Ford Foundation established the Local Initiatives Support Corporation in 1980. It grew out of the Foundation's experience over the previous decade in supporting locally-based Community Development Corporations, non-profit organisations in declining urban areas working to promote economic and physical revitalisation with considerable involvement of local residents. By the late 1970s the Foundation officials realised that the era of major federal spending on inner cities was over and a small but growing number of businesses were contributing to Community Development Corporation activities. New legislation (discussed below) put some pressure on financial institutions to make such investments.

The Foundation thought that an initiative was needed to bring together all the agencies that could contribute to urban revitalisation in effective public /private partnerships. These would be locally organised and involve business, local government, charitable foundations and the Community Development Corporations. The Local Initiatives Support Corporation was established to develop such partnerships.

In the words of Franklin Thomas, the Foundation's president and a former director of one of the largest community corporations; '*We decided to test what might be possible through a new kind of social investment vehicle – an independent, highly skilled, and well-funded intermediary organisation that would channel project money to local groups from a variety of sources. The idea was not that such an organisation would finance entire projects but that it would provide the up-front or 'glue' money to trigger locally initiated housing and commercial ventures, money that would attract and hold other investors.....In the simplest terms, the Local Initiatives Support Corporation seeks out promising Community Development Corporations and gives them technical assistance, loans, and in some cases grants, allowing them to carry out more projects and bigger projects than they would otherwise have been able to take on – and to carry them out more effectively.*'

The Support Corporation has had a considerable impact. By 1986 it had raised over $100m from around 300 companies and foundations and had assisted nearly 400 community corporations. This money has been used to attract a further $380m of public and private funding and provide over 10,000 units of new and rehabilitated housing and 2.5m sq feet of commercial and industrial space.

As the Foundation's president noted, community corporations with the backing of the Support Corporation have a particular attraction for some local authorities because '*federal domestic policies were also transforming local governments into major actors in the community development arena. To many city halls caught in the whipsaw of fewer resources and greater responsibilities community corporations...never looked so good. And for the community corporations and their other funding partners, the continued flow of public dollars, most of them now under the control of local rather than federal bodies, was nothing short of critical.*'

According to an evaluation of the Support Corporation carried out by Harvard University in 1986, it is based on the belief that, with various forms of assistance, non-profit community corporations can carry out projects which directly improve neighbourhood conditions, strengthen the group's own ability to promote physical, social and economic change and influence the '*community development community*' – that is, the network of public and private organisations which can influence neighbourhood development – to provide more resources for this purpose.

There are various elements in the strategy. First, to provide financial and technical support for particular projects involving new and rehabilitated housing and commercial and industrial property and business developments. Second, by such projects, to enable community corporations to develop the necessary skills, contacts and so on to tackle larger projects. A key element here is to help these organisations improve their financial management of projects and their resource base, so improving their chances of long-term survival.

More generally, it is believed that backing from the Support Corporation will have multiplier effects; by encouraging others to reinvest in declining areas and by providing local residents with training in running their own businesses and other organisations. The aim is to foster economic growth rather than simply redistribute existing resources. Finally, there is the impact of these activities on the 'community development community', demonstrating to other organisations that investment in such areas is possible and putting direct pressure on them to do so, especially by creating new institutional relationships or partnerships.

The Harvard report suggested that the Support Corporation's method of working falls between that which might be adopted by a banker who is only concerned with the financial returns from a project and a philanthropist only concerned with social benefits. It is concerned to make social investments which, nevertheless, are financially sound and produce economic returns, a part of which is recycled by the Support Corporation to other projects. It can also be seen as a social experiment, testing a strategy of community-based development and the associated partnerships which make this possible.

The Support Corporation was established with just under $10m, contributed by the Ford Foundation and six major companies. It concentrates its activities in a limited number of areas – 27 by 1986. Most are in the older urban centres of north-east US. These areas have local groups that want help and are able to raise local funds. The Support Corporation's financial help is given on a dollar for dollar matching basis.

According to Lawson Shadburn, an official of the Corporation whom we interviewed, the companies and foundations that donate money to the central organisation and in the local areas find these schemes attractive for several reasons. First, they can rely on the Support Corporation's expertise to select projects that have a high probability of success. Second, their money is used for a portfolio of projects, so they are seen to be supporting a wide range of schemes. Finally, they are insulated to a degree from individual requests for support from community organisations and can share with others the possible risks of adverse publicity arising from the activities of some of these organisations.

The Support Corporation concentrates on funding concrete projects and is reluctant to provide funds for general administrative support. It uses a wide variety of forms of assistance, including grants, loans (some of which are only recoverable if the project achieves a financial return) and loan guarantees. Equally important are the services which are provided: technical assistance, advice on strategy, helping to build local organisational and resource networks.

Project proposals have to be approved by the Support Corporation's headquarters staff and board of directors but the real impetus comes from the local level. In each area there are committees of the local donors who advise a locally-based programme officer. The officer helps community organisations prepare requests for assistance, sees them through the local committee which has to approve them and then through the approval at headquarters.

Shadburn told us, *'programme officers work in a very entrepreneurial way, encouraging local organisations, putting together deals by linking up organisations in co-operative arrangements and so on'*. When projects are underway the officer monitors progress and acts as a troubleshooter when problems arise.

By mid-1985 over half the Support Corporation's resources were being used to support low-income housing projects, a mixture of new building and rehabilitation but rather more of the latter. Most of these projects are fairly small, typically producing 50 to 100 units each.

Many of these are located in some of the most devastated inner city areas; for example, one larger-scale development has involved the building of 183 town houses in Cleveland's Hough neighbourhood – which had been at the centre of the urban riots of 1968; another has resulted in the rehabilitation of an 85- apartment block in the Banana-Kelly neighbourhood in New York's South Bronx, probably the USA's most blighted urban area. These projects are often very complex in two senses; first, technically, especially where rehabilitation is concerned; and second, legally and financially, as they are often financed from multiple sources. Such complexities can result in very high and essentially non-productive costs for local groups, so the Support Corporation's provision of such services is often vital. While one of the Support Corporation's main functions is to draw the private sector into community development activities, it is careful to only operate where there is positive support from local government. It will not assist community groups that are in open conflict with local officials. In many cases, public sector funding is an important element in the Support Corporation's projects; it obtains locally-allocated federal Community Development Block Grant Funds as well as – when they were available – federal Urban Development Action Grants (the latter being, incidentally, the model for British Urban Development Grants).

In several cities more permanent partnerships with local government have emerged. In Philadelphia and Chicago local officials have joined local committees of the Support Corporation and in many other locations there is collaboration on a project by project basis (the Chicago developments will be discussed later in this chapter). It also played a key role in setting up the Boston Housing Partnership which carries out large-scale rehabilitation projects, working through community housing developers and being run by a board of directors which includes public officials, directors of community development organisations and major local corporations.

The Enterprise Foundation

Another important example of a private sector initiative to channel funds into lower-income housing is the Baltimore based, but nationally active, Enterprise Foundation. It was founded in 1981 by James Rouse, one of the most successful property developers of the post-war era. Like many of the US housing organisations which we investigated, the Foundation explicitly links its housing efforts to the wider question of urban poverty and deprivation and the economic, social and political marginalisation of the poor, ' *our goal is to build a new system for housing poor families in America and to help them lift themselves out of poverty into the mainstream of American life*'.

The Foundation supplies grants and loans and opens up other credit to community-based groups involved in the low cost renovation of low-income housing. It also provides technical assistance. Initially, the Foundation was supported by contributions from charitable foundations, socially committed individuals, companies and other such sources. However, the longer term objective is to use the profits from a commercially run subsidiary which is developing 'festival marketplaces' – city markets with speciality food and clothing shops. At the time of our research, eight such projects were in construction or already being operated, including one in Australia. The Foundation was also working with the Walt Disney Company, '*to conceptualise a new type of urban-entertainment center which would combine the Disney approach to high quality entertainment with the elements of a festival marketplace*'.

There are two other subsidiaries which work on a profit making basis. The Rehab Work Group develops new methods of reducing rehabilitation and new construction costs. According to Rouse, cost reductions of 20 to 40 per cent are possible by using better technologies and reducing unnecessary regulations. The Enterprise Social Investment Corporation develops new ways of raising cheaper money for low-income housing.

The Enterprise Foundation raises cheap funds for housing in a variety of ways. In particular, the social investment corporation has established an Enterprise Loan Fund. Wealthy individuals, corporations and churches are asked to lend money at zero or very low interest rates for a term of one to five years. This money is then lent long term to aid low-income housing rehabilitation, the loans being guaranteed by the Enterprise Foundation. So the Fund borrows short and lends long. It is a revolving fund and is dependent on regular repayments of capital and (low) interest from the housing projects plus the ability to attract a continuing flow of one to five year commitments from socially motivated investors who will accept a low rate of return for limited periods.

One of the most ambitious projects which the Foundation has assisted is in the city of Chattanooga, Tennessee. Here, in collaboration with the city council, a local businessman and another foundation, a plan has been developed to rehabilitate 13,000 housing units in 26 neighbourhoods over a 10-year period. A new body, Chattanooga Neighborhood Enterprise Inc., has been formed to organise the programme and to co-ordinate efforts by the public and private sectors. This organisation will encourage and support the development of community organisations to spearhead the work and establish a low-interest revolving loan fund to provide cheap money for low-income families wishing to rehabilitate their properties and for non-profit low-income housing developers.

By the time of our research, the Foundation was active in 26 major cities across the USA on a wide variety of projects, most of which involved a combination of financial and technical assistance to coalitions of local business, local authorities and residents.

The Chicago Housing Partnership

Chicago is one of the cities which has developed a wide range of community-based groups. It exhibits all the features of increasingly polarised urban and economic development, federal and local funding, corporate and charitable involvement in housing development and so on which were outlined above. Since the mid-eighties a particularly innovative series of developments has occurred in the city which involves the private funding of lower-income housing development in conjunction with public funding. A central element of this Chicago Housing Partnership is the Chicago Equity Fund which channels corporate investment into low-income housing.

Both these initiatives arose out of developments which began in the early 1980s. According to Elspeth Revere, the director of the Woodstock Institute, a non-profit foundation which carried out research and advocacy on behalf of low-income housing, *'the key changes occurred after Harold Washington was elected as the first black mayor of the city. Much of his support came from the loose coalition of community-based groups which had grown up in the city over many years. Washington established a task force on housing which brought together community activists, non-profit local housing developers, city officials and sympathetic individuals from the private corporate, financial and property sectors. After a lot of hard work and tough bargaining this group produced a plan to combat housing abandonment and to establish a programme of new development and rehabilitation in the poorer areas of the city'.*

At the same time community groups were pressing the private sector to reinvest in the city. Two federal acts (the Community Reinvestment Act and the Home Mortgage Disclosure Act), passed in the 1970s after grassroots lobbying, allow local groups to obtain data on geographic patterns of home mortgage lending and to object to proposals for banking reorganisation (which is federally regulated).

In 1983 First National, one of the largest Chicago based banks, wanted to buy American National, another big bank. This could be prevented by the federal banking regulator if there was evidence that the banks had failed to meet the credit needs of their local communities. Thirty five neighbourhood and city-wide organisations formed the Chicago Reinvestment Alliance which objected to the takeover unless the banks increased their local investment in housing and small business enterprises. They used a unique state law which forced banks that wanted to do business with local government to disclose not just where their loans were going (as required by federal law) but where the deposits were coming from. This clearly showed that the bank was reinvesting money collected from the poorer areas of the city in better off neighbourhoods. Faced with this challenge, the bank decided to negotiate with the community groups and to concede to some of their demands.

The result was the Chicago Housing Partnership – a new strategy for channelling private finance into lower-income housing. The strategy consists of the following:-

▶ The bank agreed to provide $120m for a special loan programme to support housing and small business development. This money is only available in census tracts (the smallest area for which census data is available) where the median income is at or below 80 per cent of the metropolitan area median. Some of the money is lent at market interest rates with normal underwriting rules and some at lower rates and with more flexible lending rules. Most loans are used for rental housing development and rehabilitation by non-profit developers or by neighbourhood sponsored for-profit developers. Some loans are used for the purchase and rehabilitation of deteriorated single family housing.

The bank relies heavily on the expertise and local knowledge of neighbourhood-oriented organisations when deciding when and where to lend and for assisting in evaluating the financial viability of projects and their subsequent development. The programme is overseen by a review board consisting of six bank and six community organisation representatives.

Since this development several other banks have begun to make similar loans for community-based housing development. As the co-chair of the partnership has clearly stated, *it's not charity*. The bank lends on a commercially viable basis, using the neighbourhood organisations' services to reduce the risks which have led banks to cease lending in many deteriorated inner city areas. To make projects affordable by lower-income households, additional sources of cheaper loan and equity capital are also required.

▶ So the second main element in the Chicago strategy is a commitment from the city council to provide second mortgages at low interest rates and on a deferred repayment basis. The city uses some of its Community Development Block Grant for this purpose.

▶ The third main element in the strategy is to provide equity capital for the neighbourhood-based housing developers, the main organisations using the bank and city loans. Their work normally involves acquiring run down private rental blocks and carrying out moderate rehabilitation. One major project involved five blocks of flats in Kenwood-Oakland – described as *one of Chicago's most devastated and "disinvested" neighborhoods, with trashed empty lots, deadlands, boarded-up buildings.* Here, the partnership contributed $337,000 to $1.7m of rehabilitation costs.

The objective is to spend no more than about $15,000 dollars per unit and keep rents at levels affordable by families with incomes of between $10,000 and $15,000 per annum (1984 figures). These are not the very poorest households, who can only be housed with the addition of some federal subsidies, increasingly unavailable in the 1980s. The equity investment required is raised by another new development, the Chicago Equity Fund.

The Chicago Equity Fund

The Chicago Equity Fund also grew out of the recommendations of the community/city/private sector alliance which became known as the Chicago Housing Partnership. The equity fund encourages and enables major local companies to invest as limited partners in neighbourhood-based, lower-income housing developments. As with the loan finance programmes, this is not a charitable endeavour. As a local newspaper reported, *the companies get a return...mostly in the form of tax breaks, it's not heavy money for a big outfit but the businesslike aspect of it appears to be a selling point*. It enables investors to earn a respectable return on their money, hence making the investment something which shareholders can accept.

Brian Freeman and Barbara Beck, who worked for the Fund, told us that it is organised to reduce the risk of such investment: first, by pooling the corporate capital, so that each company's involvement is spread over several projects and second, by using the expertise of neighbourhood-based organisations to ensure that only potentially viable projects are supported. An important feature of the Fund is that the companies obtain the federal tax credits for investment in low-income housing. These meet the gap between the commercial return required on the capital (around 15 to 20 per cent in the mid-eighties) and the cost levels required to make the housing affordable for lower-income households.

The first equity fund investor partnership was formed in 1985. Thirteen companies – including several banks, local utility companies and multinationals with head offices in the city – each contributed $500,000. This money was invested as equity in $26m dollars worth of rehabilitation projects in lower-income areas, amounting in all to over 500 apartments. In 1986 a new partnership funded over 400 rehabilitated rental units. Most of this housing was also supported with Chicago Housing Partnership bank and city mortgages.

The programme only provides a small amount of affordable housing, compared with the overall need in the city. But in comparison with what was previously being built, it has had a significant impact. For example, before the equity fund and the other developments the neighbourhood housing developers had only produced about 200 units a year and, with the curtailment of federal support for new building and rehabilitation, few other sources of new and rehabilitated lower-income housing now exist.

The availability of skilled technical assistance is essential for the success of the equity fund, as well as all other attempts to channel private investment into lower-income housing in inner city areas. It helps neighbourhood-based developers to prepare proposals which the investors will accept; deals with financial, legal and other questions; and monitors the developments as they proceed. The Chicago Housing Partnership provides such expertise as well as lobbying for further corporate support.

A specialist non-profit support organisation, the Community Equity Assistance Corporation, was formed at the same time as the equity fund. This was initiated and supported by the Local Initiatives Support Corporation which obtained money from Chicago business and charitable sources to set it up. It is hoped that the organisation will become self-financing through the modest fees which it charges project developers for its technical services (these are far below those charged by private sector firms doing similar project development work).

The Community Equity Assistance Corporation helps to prepare project budgets, to obtain project financing from public and private sources, and to establish the partnership arrangements required to gain the private sector equity investment. It recommends suitable builders, architects, lawyers and so on and assists with project accounting (especially complex when investment partnerships are involved in development).

So in response to the declining opportunities for public funding, a linked set of organisations has been developed in Chicago to channel private sector funds into housing. By 1986 the Ford Foundation was convinced of the viability of these methods of encouraging corporate investment in lower-income housing. Early in 1987 it launched, through the Local Initiatives Support Corporation, a National Equity Fund to obtain corporate capital for a national investment programme and for the necessary technical expertise.

It is also eventually meant to be self-financing. Investors will receive the federal tax credits. These run for 10 years and amount each year to between four and nine per cent of project costs. Eligible projects have to allocate 20 to 40 per cent of their units to families on no more than around half of the area median income; rents must not exceed 30 per cent of eligible family income levels (including utilities). Given standards now accepted in the US, such rents are regarded as 'reasonable'. Rents have to be maintained at this level for 15 years.

Businesses contribute to the equity fund over six to seven years; this extended period is necessary for acceptable returns to be obtained. Eventually the equity amounts to about 25 per cent. National Equity Fund will handle all aspects of the investment, including the collection of instalments from the companies and the payments to projects. It will also arrange short term bridging finance to cover the period while the equity investment is building up, borrowing from the banks or the Local Initiatives Support Corporation and repaying these lenders as the equity payments are received.

The South Shore Bank

These Chicago initiatives have attracted national attention and have led to a national programme modelled on their experience. There are also several other different kinds of innovative approaches to increasing the flow of private capital into lower-income housing.

One example, also from Chicago, is the South Shore Bank. In this case a private sector financial institution has taken the initiative in supporting neighbourhood revitalisation and housing development. South Shore is an area of Chicago which, in the 1960s and 1970s, went through the typical process of decline of many US inner city areas. Economic decline was accompanied by a rapid racial transition in its population. In 1960 it was a wholly white area; by 1974, 95 per cent of its residents were black. In 1969 the median income of residents was nine per cent higher than the national median, by 1978 it was only 74 per cent of the national level. Retail and other businesses were in rapid decline, as was the housing stock. Abandonment of both housing and business premises was spreading.

Nevertheless, the area did contain a considerable number of better paid, skilled, manual and white collar workers who could potentially use conventional sources of mortgage credit to improve their housing situation. The problem was that institutions were reluctant to lend in an area which was declining so rapidly. Of course, this reluctance to lend simply accelerated the process of decline.

South Shore had a local bank which had, for many years, provided credit for local firms and mortgage loans for small landlords and owner-occupiers. By the early 1970s the bank had become unprofitable and it was announced that it was to be sold and relocated in the downtown area. A local community organisation objected, claiming that the move would further undermine the viability of the area. The regulatory authorities accepted the objection and refused to permit relocation. The bank was then bought by a group of investors who aimed to use it to promote inner city revitalisation, combining this social objective with profitable commercial business. According to Mary Houghton, who runs the bank's revitalisation programmes, '...*the primary purpose is to pursue a unique approach to neighborhood development and renewal. We have a system that is profit-based, that has the capacity to grow*'.

James Fletcher, the bank's president, told us that it is now owned by a general holding company which has several subsidiaries. First, there is the South Shore Bank itself, which operates according to commercial criteria and is subject to the normal bank regulatory regime. In addition, there are a number of development-oriented, for-profit and non-profit subsidiaries. These carry out activities in which the bank cannot be directly involved for legal and financial reasons. The companies are run by interlocking boards of directors on which there are representatives of the foundations, churches, corporations and individuals that have invested in the bank. Their motives for investing in the bank vary but, while most seek a reasonable long term return on their capital, they are also committed to its social objectives.

Two of the bank's affiliates, one of them a for-profit organisation, provide small business finance. Another non-profit organisation, wholly funded from public and charitable sources, provides job training, including the skills required for housing rehabilitation. It also supplies technical assistance to neighbourhood housing developers and individual owners. The board of this organisation has a majority membership of local residents. Finally, there is a for-profit housing development organisation which buys and rehabilitates run-down rental property. This is directly controlled by the main holding company.

The bank makes loans for owner occupation and to support private rental housing. In the latter case, it requires landlords purchasing property to carry out some rehabilitation, thus ensuring that stock does get upgraded. Essentially, the bank applies normal criteria when judging the eligibility of applicants for loan finance but, unlike other lenders, it believes that the area will revive rather than decline further. It does not regard the changed racial composition of the area as increasing the riskiness of lending, or discriminate against women applicants. The bank is also less inclined than other banks to apply rigid formulae relating loan amounts to income. In short, the bank is more flexible than other lenders, is not put off lending by the type of area concerned and uses its local knowledge to best advantage. In addition, it concentrates its loans for rental housing in certain localities so there is an area-wide impact.

An interesting feature of the bank is that it not only obtains normal deposits from the public but has successfully attracted so called 'development deposits' by national advertising which stresses that investors will earn a commercial return and help to support social development activities. By the time we did our research, about one third of the bank's $110m deposits came from this source. At this point the bank was providing a wide range of credit facilities, all of which were aimed at sustaining the development of the area.

Thus, apart from its support for housing rehabilitation projects, it also made improvement loans to existing homeowners, small business loans, loans to assist community organisations and loans to meet college fees. In 1985 it lent about $8.6m, of which by far the largest amount, $5.1m, was for the acquisition and rehabilitation of 31 parcels of rented property. One indicator of the bank's success was that its loans were beginning to be accepted in the secondary mortgage market, allowing the bank to release further funds for lending in the area.

Apart from these activities, supported directly by the bank's commercial lending, its two housing affiliates are also active. The non-profit affiliate, the Neighborhood Institute, concentrates on housing and job training programmes. In 1985 it had developed about 45 housing units, some for rental and some for co-operative ownership, and was just starting its largest project yet, the rehabilitation of a large and very badly deteriorated block for low and moderate-income households.

The profit motivated developer, City Lands Corporation, was using federal subsidies to build housing on which it could earn normal developer's fees but which was for occupancy by lower-income households. In 1985 it completed just over 60 units and had another 130 under construction. It was also developing a shopping plaza to 'anchor' other developments supported by the bank in a formerly declining local business centre. Apart from its other benefits and the profits which it would make, the plaza would provide new jobs for low-income local residents. In all, the bank and its affiliates were supporting about $15m worth of housing investment in the area in 1985, partly through the activities of its affiliates and partly through its normal commercial loans for private owners and community housing organisations.

The federal government carried out an assessment of the bank in the early 1980s. It concluded that sound banking business and good customers were to be found in lower-income, predominantly minority areas, such as South Shore; that a bank could operate profitably in such circumstances; and that normal banking business could be combined with community development subsidiaries to undertake riskier endeavours and serve lower-income residents without impairing its profitability. Finally, the report noted that there was some hard evidence, for example a reversal of declining property values, to suggest that a positive impact was being made on the neighbourhood by the bank's efforts.

The Baltimore Housing Partnership

In many cases, as we have noted, the initial impetus for public/private/community partnerships has come from organisations like the Local Initiatives Support Corporation or from community-based organisations that have subsequently formed closer links with local government in their areas. One reason for this may be that most American cities do not have housing departments which have the sort of broad responsibility for local housing that is normal in Britain. In most cases, for example, public housing is run by public housing authorities which are separate from the local council.

However, there are a few exceptions to this rule. One of them is Baltimore. Here, public housing is directly run by the local authority which also has a long history of other housing activities, especially in relation to rehabilitation. Baltimore was, for example, one of the first cities to develop area-based rehabilitation, bringing together community groups, the city and mortgage institutions for specific projects. It also pioneered urban homesteading together with a few other cities in the 1970s.

Peter Matthews, the assistant director of the Partnership, explained to us that the Baltimore Housing Partnership began in 1984 when the city's mayor (who later became the state Governor) approached the local business community to establish a programme to acquire and rehabilitate vacant housing, reduce costs and develop new financing methods so that the housing would be affordable by moderate-income households. This initiative was a response to the withdrawal of federal government funding of such programmes – which had been accompanied by a call for local government and the private sector to take its place. As Matthews said, 'we're proud that *every one of our projects has been done without any sort of government assistance, write-down or grant. We're trying to meet the call to fill in where the government has withdrawn in housing initiatives'.*

So the Baltimore scheme, unlike the Chicago partnership, aims to produce affordable housing without using subsidies (apart from certain tax reliefs). It is essentially an attempt to develop a commercially run organisation – with some public sector support and links to community-based organisations – which makes housing available to moderate-income households on the best possible terms.

When the Housing Partnership was founded, Baltimore had about 5,000 units of abandoned housing and many more units which were deteriorating. Many of these houses were located in formerly stable inner city areas and were a source of blight, contributing to the decline which threatened such areas. Often, these houses had been owned by private landlords. However, Baltimore has a high level of working class owner-occupation, especially in some strongly demarcated, white immigrant, working class inner city neighbourhoods, where very active community organisations have arisen in the past few years. Typically, and rather unusually for the USA, much of Baltimore's older inner city housing stock consists of small row (terrace) houses, which can be easily converted for low cost home ownership.

Given this background, many city rehabilitation programmes have provided housing for moderate-income owner-occupation. Baltimore Housing Partnership follows this pattern. According to Matthews, it has several key objectives;

▶ To involve the local business and civic community in its development activities;

▶ To attract private capital to finance housing;

▶ To promote neighbourhood stabilisation by developing home ownership opportunities. Where this is not immediately possible, then to provide a system for educating and training residents in preparation for home ownership;

▶ To develop programmes to acquire and renovate vacant properties;

▶ To establish creative financing techniques which increase the funding for housing production and sales;

▶ To produce affordable housing;

▶ To encourage the development industry to contribute to the Partnership.

The partnership consists of two companies, the Baltimore Corporation for

Housing Partnerships, a non-profit organisation which can receive charitable donations (under US law such donations are tax deductible) and which also received an initial grant of working capital from the city council. This has a fully owned profit-making subsidiary, the Baltimore Housing Partnership Development Corporation, which acquires the houses, carries out the renovations and then sells the units to first time buyers. All development profits accrue to the Baltimore Corporation for Housing Partnerships which re-lends the money to finance new developments. One option for the future is for the profit-making subsidiary to branch out into up-market developments, increasing the profits which it will then be able to channel into moderate-income housing production.

Baltimore Corporation for Housing Partnerships lends to its subsidiary at near market rates of interest but the sale prices of the housing are well below what a normal commercial developer would charge. Advantageous mortgage terms are also available. An important factor which reduces costs is that this housing is eligible for city and state loans at lowered interest rates. This finance comes from the sale of tax free bonds, as described earlier in this chapter. At the time of the research households with incomes of less than $20,000 per year could also have their sales taxes and other transaction costs covered by this loan (and these expenses are very high in the city).

A loan could be obtained at seven per cent with only $1,000 down payment (for those on higher incomes, up to $33,000, the terms were less generous but still attractive). This compared with market interest rates of around 10 per cent. A further cost saving is that the houses only have basic work done to them, they are made structurally sound and only necessary repairs carried out. As Matthews states, '...what we try to do is build the basics – something that is sanitary and affordable, which means forgoing luxury'. In addition, the Baltimore Housing Partnership forms joint ventures with private developers who are expected to reduce their profit margins and fees. Finally, the profits which flow back to the non-profit subsidiary allow some cross subsidy of the loan terms offered to those eligible households which had the lowest acceptable incomes. It is intended that in time the Baltimore Housing Partnership will become self-supporting, covering all its costs from sales revenue.

The Partnership obtains its houses in various ways: sometimes they are offered for sale by landlords and sometimes vacant abandoned units can be bought at auction sales (having been taken over by the city in lieu of unpaid property taxes). Before deciding to buy, the Housing Partnership examines the local level of market prices and estimates the cost of rehabilitation.

Unlike the Chicago operation, the Partnership does not work through community-based housing developers. It operates like a conventional developer, although community organisations sometimes put it in touch with eligible buyers. In some cases, we were told, the Partnership had come into conflict with neighbourhood groups, especially in white areas where the new occupants were black and racism raised its head. On the whole, the Partnership does not work in the poorest areas of the city but in relatively better off but slowly declining working class neighbourhoods. In fact, a central objective is to stabilise such areas, to prevent them becoming increasingly occupied by the poorest households and to deal with vacant abandoned properties.

A serious problem is that the cost of acquiring and rehabilitating a house often means that its selling price was above predominant local market prices (that is, there is a 'valuation gap'). This is another reason why the cost of work has to be kept as low as possible. In 1986 the partnership aimed to produce housing for no more than $48,000. This would be affordable by households earning $17,000 to $25,000 per year. One of the cheaper projects, called the Shipley Hill Condominiums, involved the conversion of two nineteenth-century houses into six units. These were sold for between $36,500 and $44,900, making them affordable for people with incomes between $16,000 and $19,000 a year.

In comparison with the Chicago partnership, it is aiming at distinctly better off households, essentially those who can just about afford to move out of rental housing and into ownership without heavy subsidies but with a little assistance from cheaper finance and easy purchase terms. One advantage of the Baltimore Partnership's decision not to use direct subsidies is that it does not have to meet the fairly high standards for rehabilitation which are a condition of such subsidies and which add to costs, thus reducing affordability. Such subsidies normally have to be repaid if the homeowner decides to sell; the Partnership's houses do not carry any such requirements.

Baltimore Housing Partnership is run by an ex-city housing official with a small staff. Its board of directors includes representatives of major financial and property interests in the city – its chairman is the chief executive of the locally-important Union Trust Bank – and two of the larger community-based organisations. Considerable attention is paid to screening buyers to make sure that they can afford the housing and to marketing. Some properties have been hard to sell because of the basic level of rehabilitation and the prices are often rather high in relation to local market levels. The Partnership's achievements at the time of our research were modest in comparison with the Chicago partnership. Its target was to rehabilitate about 75 houses a year. Given the nature of what it was attempting, to sell to marginal buyers in the less attractive areas of the city, this low target was hardly surprising.

The Mount Vernon Apartment Improvement Program

So far we have been discussing innovative projects which mainly operate in the inner areas of large cities. However, another project which we visited is located in Mount Vernon, a smaller city a few miles north-east of New York City. Christine Hylton, the Mount Vernon Apartment Improvement Program director describes the area in which it works thus: '*The Mount Vernon neighborhood was developed in the early part of this century. Part of the neighborhood, Bailey Estates, was the home of the circus entrepreneurs, H.Barnum and Bailey. The area is now comprised of gracious single-family homes in the $200,000 and up range as well as 18 large 35–200 unit apartment buildings. Situated in the north-east section of Mount Vernon, the area consists of 65 per cent non-minority and 35 per cent minority upper-middle, middle-income and low-to-moderate income families*'.

In the 1970s there was concern about neighbourhood decline. The most serious problem involved the rental blocks. It was alleged that state rent controls and low tenant incomes meant that rents failed to cover landlords' costs and provide a return on their investment. This resulted in a run down of maintenance and increasing dereliction – often compounded by poor management. The programme was set up in 1979 to rehabilitate these properties while maintaining rents at an affordable level for their existing tenants. The Program's stated goal is '*To preserve neighborhood stability and desirability as a place to live, and provide decent, attractive housing for Mount Vernon's many tenant residents*'.

The programme was established with support from the Neighborhood Reinvestment Corporation (see chapter two). Mount Vernon was one of two sites chosen by the Corporation to pilot a new approach to rental rehabilitation which had been pioneered, as a purely local initiative, in another city in the state of New York, Yonkers. The Corporation provided administrative funding and technical assistance. The city council also contributed towards these costs, using federal Community Development Block Grant funds. Initially, the programme only used conventional finance. Later, it used some further block grant funds together with private investment and loans to keep costs down. By the mid-eighties the Mount Vernon programme had renovated over 700 units. Its efforts had been complemented by environmental and service improvements carried out by the city council.

The Apartment Improvement Program is a non-profit organisation. It has a small, paid staff. Its directors include representatives of the interested parties – lenders, community organisations, the tenants of the buildings, their landlords and city officials – each being equally represented on the policy making board. There are are subcommittees dealing with fund raising, the selection of buildings and the evaluation of whether they can be successfully rehabilitated.

Like most of the projects discussed so far in this chapter, the Mount Vernon programme improves property that is not so seriously deteriorated that it can only be rescued by very large-scale investment. Keeping costs to a minimum is essential if existing tenants are to be retained. At the same time, the landlords retain their properties and gain a return from their operation. Each building develops tenant support organisations, provides information on what repairs are required, helps to establish and maintain tenancy and building condition standards and screens potential new tenants.

The landlords provide financial information about the buildings, are responsible for carrying through management and physical improvements and for following the improvement plans for the buildings which have been agreed by the partnerships. The financial institutions supply financial expertise and often provide new loans or restructure existing mortgages. Local government supports the Program staff and carries out environmental improvements, as already noted, and also reduces property tax assessments.

Like the Baltimore Housing Partnership, the Mount Vernon Program tries to avoid reliance on subsidies (although in a few cases this has been necessary). So the emphasis is on rehabilitation to minimal standards; efficiency of operations, including subsequent management; and financing arrangements which are the most advantageous that can be obtained from the private sector. As the buildings remain in the ownership of their landlords (although in some cases they prefer to sell out, in which case the Program finds new landlords to take them over), it is the landlords who borrow the money for improvements. Therefore, rents have to be increased to meet the increased debt charges. The aim is to pay off the costs of the rehabilitation within five years. It is hoped that the landlords will then reduce rents, although there is no compulsion to do this, and apparently little likelihood that they will do so!

On average about $3,000 is spent on each apartment – but in some cases as much as $10,000. Despite this modest expenditure, Mount Vernon projects have apparently made a big impact on their localities, encouraging substantial rises in house prices and general upgrading. This has encouraged the banks to lend to landlords belonging to the Program. Other important inducements are that the Program provides financial plans and skilled appraisals of the rehabilitation needs of the properties. Left to themselves, the small landlords who own the properties cannot prepare such professional and competent plans for presentation to the banks.

One example of a Mount Vernon project, which illustrates its methods, concerned a 30 year old, 203-unit, six-storey block. Before rehabilitation units rented on average for $73 per week. The owner was making a loss on the property. About $450,000 was spent on rehabilitation, mainly on repairs but also on kitchen improvements and some landscaping. The city reduced the building's tax assessment, under a programme which allows reductions when landlords spend money on repairs and improvements. This saved the landlord $63,000 dollars a year. In addition, the tenants agreed to a modest rent increase, up to $85 per week (still under the local average of $90 per week). A new mortgage was arranged to replace the existing mortgage and provide an extra $350,000 towards the improvement costs. The owner provided the other $100,000. These changes resulted in a positive cash flow. With various other considerations, including the ability of the owner to claim a depreciation allowance against his federal tax payments, the return in the first year after improvement was almost $80,000, or 15.5 per cent of the owner's equity investment.

Christine Hylton admitted that one obvious problem was that by upgrading the area, prices and therefore costs for lower-income residents are rising. However, she rejected our suggestion that gentrification might result; most tenants were protected by a non-eviction plan. One limitation, already referred to, was that the project only worked in the less deteriorated areas of Mount Vernon. She told us that the mostly black, low-income families living in the southern part of Mount Vernon were living in much worse conditions. *'The buildings are much more neglected. There is a high turnover in building ownership. This increases the mortgage debt and leaves little for maintenance and improvement. Landlords have insufficient cash flow to back an application for a bank loan'.*

Discussion

If one compares the achievements of the innovatory developments described in this chapter with the scale of housing needs, it is clear that even the Chicago programmes are only making a very limited impact. Certainly, there is no indication that private sector resources can entirely replace the public support which has been withdrawn over the past few years (and even this was on a modest scale compared with the size of the housing problem in inner city areas).

However, in a situation where there is no alternative, private sector finance as well as the professional and development skills of the property industry can be attracted into providing some housing which is more affordable than similar quality units which are offered on the open market. But the circumstances where it can work are very limited and need to be carefully noted. There are a number of key considerations:-

▶ Only very limited amounts of finance are available at a really low cost. In most cases, banks and other corporations spend little on purely charitable causes. Such funds may be useful, for example, in providing supplementary finance or helping to establish technical service organisations but they are insufficient to support even quite modest housing development programmes. Therefore, the first essential is that private sector capital earns a commercial rate of return. Obviously, the level of return which is regarded as commercially acceptable varies: in the case of the Chicago Equity Fund, as we noted, it amounted to 15 to 20 per cent. In the case of the South Shore Bank, the federal study of its operations concluded that 'profit maximising venture capitalists' would not be interested in a similar operation but that institutions prepared to limit themselves to a 'reasonable' rate of return could be attracted to it.

▶ Requiring a commercial rate of return has important consequences for what can be achieved. Essentially, there is a trade off between financial viability and commercial objectives. Quite where the balance is struck varies, depending on the circumstances of each project. If the project can obtain subsidies or especially cheap property to rehabilitate, the cost of housing can be reduced. However, in each of the projects which we examined it was made clear to us that without some public subsidies the housing was not affordable by those on the lowest incomes.

In practice, this normally means that groups with a moderate – but not those with a very low-income are being served. For example, in Chicago and other areas the rents were affordable by households with incomes around 60 to 80 per cent of the area median. Our impression is that most schemes were targeted at households in the $12,000 to $25,000 a year range. For rough comparative purposes, it is worth noting that in 1985 the federal government estimated that a poverty-level income (that is, excluding possible non-monetary welfare and other benefits) for a four person household was around $11,000. A little more than a fifth of households had incomes at or below this level. At the same date, the median household money income was about $24,000.

▶ Even to achieve these levels of affordability requires considerable effort on the part of housing developers and their advisors. First, the emphasis is on moderate rehabilitation to basic standards. Severely deteriorated properties are not viable propositions; as the director of the National Equity Fund notes, 'we don't go into the most bombed-out areas'. Second, properties also have to be relatively cheap to buy. This means, for example, that developers cannot work in areas where gentrification is underway and market prices are rising (although, as we saw in the case of Mount Vernon, the projects themselves may help to bring about gentrification). It is also necessary to economise on the costs of professional services, hence the importance of non-profit technical assistance organisations.

▶ A further consequence of the need to keep costs down is that it is usually necessary to combine various forms of funding: conventional commercial loans; supplementary loans at lower rates of interest, perhaps from a city or state government, or a revolving loan fund; and tax subsidised equity investment. In most cases, this results in very complex financial and legal arrangements which are difficult and time consuming to put together and potentially very expensive. As the director of the Baltimore partnership has commented, 'each property has its own little soap opera'. Again, the value of the specialist intermediary organisations linking the housing developers and sources of finance is evident.

▶ Although the role of local government as a provider of financial assistance is now much reduced, it still has a key function in this respect and more generally, via its regulative powers and in other ways, is regarded as an essential participant in enabling developments to occur. Organisations such as the Enterprise Foundation and the Local Initiatives Support Corporation think that it is not worthwhile trying to operate where the local authorities are hostile or even indifferent to their work.

▶ In a few cases, notably the Baltimore Housing Partnership, the programme is close to a normally run private sector operation. In other cases, the role of neighbourhood-based housing developers or other local bodies is far more important. However, the extent to which even these programmes are neighbourhood *initiated* and *controlled* rather than neighbourhood-*based*, with some representation of local notables among their directorates, varies a good deal. Likewise, the extent to which the housing which results is tenant controlled or is run by the developer as a landlord also varies a good deal. The Local Initiatives Support Corporation officials told us that neighbourhood housing developers were having to become more entrepreneurial and professional in their work, as they could no longer obtain much public funding and were having to go to the private sector.

The Chicago Housing Partnership officials told us that this had led to some tension, especially in groups which have evolved out of grassroots protest organisations and which still retain campaigning objectives. There can also be other sources of tension. For example, in Chicago some groups wanted to use local contractors and professionals, despite the lack of proven capacity of such firms to handle complex and expensive projects.

▶ Given these difficulties one might wonder just why it seems to all concerned so important that development should occur through neighbourhood-based organisations. In part, this simply happens to be how the situation has developed. For groups with a commitment to the preservation of their localities a movement into physical and economic development activities, especially in the absence of effective government action, is an obvious step to take.

More significantly from the point of view of private investors, many such groups have the detailed local knowledge and organisation to see developments through and subsequently monitor them. This enables investors to minimise their risks. In this context, the neighbourhood housing developers are taking the place of the small local landlords who also used local knowledge and personal management to ensure that their investments remained viable.

▶ This raises a more general point concerning the value of involving locally-based organisations with technical and other skills if significant private sector capital is to be attracted to lower-income housing. Many financial institutions and most non-property oriented corporate investors do not have the in–house capacity to assess which properties are viable propositions, work up development briefs and arrange the financial and legal aspects of these operations, screen individual borrowers to see whether they can meet repayment obligations, negotiate with multiple sources of finance and so on.

The availability of neighbourhood housing developers and the various technical support organisations enables these functions to be carried out effectively, so reducing the costs and the risks of private sector investment in lower-income housing. At the same time these organisations provide the institutional base for advocacy and entrepreneurial initiative on behalf of lower-income housing needs, pressing the private sector for funding and showing it how it can make a contribution while still obtaining a commercial return.

▶ One possible source of funds for lower-income housing which a number of projects, such as the Enterprise Foundation and the South Shore Bank, were trying to establish, was profit making development subsidiaries. In addition, most programmes aim at achieving, over time, a fairly high degree of self-sufficiency, covering their core costs from their revenue, although often being prepared to use subsidies for individual schemes where these were available. While this limits what they can achieve in terms of affordability, it does mean that they are not wholly dependent for their future existence on an increasingly limited and uncertain flow of government assistance.

▶ Another promising development, just beginning to be exploited, was the use of the secondary mortgage market. As we noted, the South Shore Bank had been able to sell some of its mortgages, thus releasing funds for further lending. In 1986 the Local Initiatives Support Corporation established the Local Initiatives Managed Assets Corporation to act as a national secondary market for Community Development Corporation project loans. With $9m initial funding from the Ford Foundation and other foundation and corporate investors, the new corporation aimed to buy a portfolio of the best performing Community Development Corporation loans from lenders, releasing money for new developments.

To summarise, the attraction of private sector finance and development skills into lower-income housing is no easy task. It remains to be seen just how large a contribution they will make in increasing the supply of decent and affordable housing in the poorer urban areas. Opinions about their value differ. Thus an article in the Wall Street Journal (10 December 1986) reported that some experts felt that the new programmes were '*too little, too late to cure America's urban ills...these efforts are good for the psyches of boards of directors of foundations...(but) the multiplier effect of community development organisations is small and their contagion has yet to be proven*'. In response, the Mayor of Boston, Raymond Flynn, commented, '*the national policy we now have is no policy at all... urban policy for the remainder of this century and beyond will be collaboration of community groups, local government and business*'.

However, without some public subsidies, private finance is unable to provide housing for those on the lowest incomes. Even in relation to rather better off groups great care has to be taken to minimise costs. One consequence is that areas where the housing is severely deteriorated – or where 'normal' market processes are leading to a revival of property values – have to be avoided. Finally, most schemes are far more complex in their organisation and finances than conventional developments in either the private or the public sectors. So the contribution of professional and technical skills, available at relatively low cost, is essential.

5. ► Extending Home Ownership

T he extension of home ownership to lower-income households, especially in inner city areas, has been a policy objective of successive British governments. In the 1970s there was considerable interest in shared equity schemes. After 1979 the government supported several other initiatives, including improvement for sale and schemes which involved the provision of cheap land and public/private sector partnerships.

Few of these programmes have made much impact. The only major exception is the sale of council housing. Yet in spite of increasing discounts to tempt council tenants to buy their homes, by the mid-eighties the volume of sales was declining.

The 1988 Housing Act marked something of a switch of emphasis for Mrs Thatcher's government, in that it was mainly concerned with a diversification and renewal of the private rental sector. But the government's major interest continues to be owner-occupation.

In this chapter we will examine some of the innovatory attempts to expand moderate-income home ownership which have been adopted in other countries and assess their successes and failures. We have already referred to one such project, the Baltimore Housing Partnership, but this was only operating on a small scale. In this chapter we concentrate on two much more ambitious projects, both located in New York City, and refer to developments in the Netherlands and West Germany.

The down-market extension of home ownership by innovatory programmes is less common in these latter two countries than in the USA. In part this is because, in both the Netherlands and West Germany, there have been long established 'mainstream' direct subsidy programmes to support the production of new, moderate-income, owner-occupied housing. In addition, home ownership, as we saw in chapter one, is less extensive in these countries than it is in either Britain or the USA, so it is hardly surprising that they have made less effort to develop low cost home ownership initiatives.

The Nehemiah Plan

The Nehemiah Plan is a project to develop new low cost owner-occupied housing in East Brooklyn, one of the most devastated areas of New York City. From the 1950s East Brooklyn became an area – like the more famous, or notorious, South Bronx – where poor black and Hispanic households found cheap rental housing. A rapid racial transition occurred as in many US inner cities at this time. Property rapidly deteriorated as landlord disinvestment occurred, many buildings were abandoned, arson was widespread (initiated by landlords wishing to 'liquidate' their investments via insurance claims) and extensive tracts of vacant land appeared. Apart from the physical deterioration of the area, it became a dangerous place to live as crime, often linked to drug dealing, escalated. Retail facilities and other sources of employment and services closed down. In the 1970s, as the city's fiscal crisis developed, this was one of the areas where even basic public service provision collapsed.

In short, it is an area which had largely been written off as irredeemable by the public authorities and politicians (the term 'planned shrinkage' was coined to describe such officially abandoned areas). By the early 1980s a local paper described the site on which the first Nehemiah Plan housing was to be built in these words, '*Twenty-six publicly owned high rises and some medium rises, mostly low-income, provide the only occupied housing....today. Eleven thousand families look out from...public housing buildings on a sad landscape of lots filled with broken bricks and shoulder high weeds and a few still standing vacant buildings. They live in a neighborhood of high unemployment and high crime, poor health and low voter participation*'.

The Nehemiah Plan is a remarkable attempt to reverse such conditions by means of new housing development. The Plan was initiated by local church-based organisations, virtually the only remaining organisations with roots in the local population, according to Mike Gecan, a worker with the project who we interviewed. These bodies, using money raised from their members and charitable sources, had already taken the lead in combating the decline of the area. They helped to provide new retail facilities, campaigned for increased police protection for residents and to drive drug dealing out of the neighbourhood. They were involved in job creation for young people and in the improvement of transport facilities. Housing was just one of the church-sponsored activities in the area.

The Nehemiah Plan began in the early 1980s. It aimed to construct 5,000 new single family row (terrace) houses on vacant and devastated sites to accommodate black, Hispanic and white households who cannot normally afford to buy. The target group earns $20,000 to $40,000 a year. The project's sponsor is East Brooklyn Churches, a federation of 52 local churches. The project also employs the Industrial Areas Foundation, a professional group which assists localities in the development of an effective political voice by training local leadership and establishing community organisations. In addition, the project is aided by funding from major religious denominations and by the private sector which gives expert advice. Finally, the project would not have been possible without the active support of local and national politicians.

These have been most effectively lobbied by the project sponsors, backed up by grassroots support. What this involves was illustrated by a report for the New York housing activists' magazine *City Limits* about an on-site meeting to initiate the project. The reporter wrote, '*It was a housing activist's dream, five thousand people standing together on inner city land hitherto "planned" only for urban shrinkage, a vast prairie stretching just beyond the edge of a housing project...five thousand people, mostly black and low-income, holding hands with the mayor, city council president, housing commissioner, and borough president, focused together in the peculiar concentration of prayer as a minister intones, "Be Thou unto us a tower of strength to those who would put obstacles in our path"*'. One obvious power which the churches have is to rally many of their more middle class and politically vocal congregations behind the project.

According to the churches, the Nehemiah Plan offers an alternative to the fate of many other low-income inner city areas in the USA. In many cities poor households have to live in deteriorating and dangerous private rental blocks; or, less frequently, are rehoused in high density, high rise subsidised projects; or are squeezed out as middle class gentrification results in the physical renovation of areas but also their social, economic and racial transition.

The plan provides a fourth alternative for some of these households. The belief is that by developing low cost home ownership, rather than rental housing, it will meet the aspirations of many poorer households – to escape from landlord operated, high density flat living – and give them a real stake in the area. This will help to recreate a stable community and reverse disintegration and decline. So Nehemiah involves much more than housing development – it is part of a wide ranging effort to rebuild the local economy and community. As one of the churches' representatives put it at the meeting which *City Limits* reported on, '*We are more than a Nehemiah Plan, we are about the central development of dignity and self-respect. All our projects, including Nehemiah, are only a means to that end*'.

Great emphasis is placed on increasing the impact that local residents can have on public and private sectors by community organising and lobbying for resources. The Brooklyn churches realise that the political empowerment of localities such as East Brooklyn is an essential precondition for their revival, because this can only occur if the city and other authorities reverse their policies of disinvestment in the area. According to *City Limits*, '*even the meekest of the pastors involved*' refer to the importance of working together in a '*power organisation*'.

The churches' organisation is supported by regular donations from the members of local church congregations, but housing development requires far more finance than it can raise locally. However, a number of potential resources are available. First, there is a supply of vacant land and land on which there are only derelict buildings. Second, the basic infrastructure – roads, sewers and utilities – is already in place, so these development costs do not have to be incurred. Third, there are other facilities such as schools, subways and shops. Finally, there are the church organisations themselves, actively working in the area.

The resulting plan is based on an idea which had been canvassed by I. D. Robbins, a well known former private developer. Robbins argued for the creation of large, new housing developments in the inner cities, along the lines of the highly successful homeowner suburbs that speculative developers had built throughout the US after the second world war, and which, with the aid of federal mortgage insurance, had opened up suburban home ownership to a great mass of the middle-income population.

He claimed that most government programmes for inner city housing were costly, over bureaucratic ('*run by club house hacks*') and ineffective. Moreover, they usually resulted in high rise, high density rental housing which was unpopular with residents and soon fell into neglect and disrepair. He was also opposed to large-scale rehabilitation, suggesting that new build projects would be cheaper in the long run and contribute more to neighbourhood stabilisation. These views had not endeared him to many community-based organisations or to local politicians and officials. Nevertheless, Robbins became a consultant to East Brooklyn Churches. His plan is based on a number of key requirements. These are:

▶ Developments should be on a large scale: small projects will be doomed to failure as they will make little impact on the areas in which they are located;

▶ The housing must be low rise, single family owner-occupied units. An East Brooklyn Churches survey has shown that this was what local households desired. Also, such housing is up to 50 per cent cheaper to build than high rise blocks and, it is believed, will help to bring about safer neighbourhoods and a more stable social structure.

▶ Control over the design, quality of construction and scale of the project must be retained by the churches, in other words, by representatives of the locality, rather than being taken over by private developers or government agencies. The latter, it is believed, would only impose their own requirements at the expense of those desired by local residents.

▶ Financial support from the state and local governments is required.

▶ The project has to employ efficient building firms to ensure tight schedules and prompt payments to subcontractors. Otherwise, the quality of the building will suffer, as well as the effort to minimise costs.

▶ Homes have to be affordable by local residents.

▶ All homes have to be pre-sold to minimise costs.

▶ A revolving loan fund must be created by the churches to provide interest free construction finance.

East Brooklyn Churches has followed a carefully thought out strategy of building up political commitment to and resources for its plan. First, the local Catholic bishop, Francis Mugavero, took the lead in creating the revolving fund, initially obtaining over $6m from three major denominations. This fund is only used to finance the works during construction, being replenished as the houses are sold. A cost reduction of six to seven per cent results. Once this fund was established, the churches and their consultant lobbied Mayor Koch of New York to obtain city assistance. This resulted in $10 million of interest free loan capital. According to Bishop Mugavero, 'at first the bureaucrats thought that we were whacko. The mayor said he didn't have the money. Finally, I looked at him and I said, "I'll tell you what: you steal the money and I'll absolve you". He looked at me and said, "You've got it"'.

The city also agreed to provide the land for the houses, free of charge (most of the vacant lots, the sites of abandoned buildings, come into city ownership through property tax arrears proceedings). On average the cost to the city of clearing these sites is about $3,000. The city loan allows each unit to receive a $10,000 non-repayable, no interest loan, in effect a charge on the property only repayable when the owner moves out. In the first project area the average cost of the housing was reduced to $43,500 as a result of this loan. The city also agreed to exempt the units from all property taxes for 10 years and to repair streets, sewers and other infrastructure.

Having established the revolving loan fund and obtained the city commitment, the churches were able to go to the state governor with these assets and obtain access to long term state mortgage finance at a preferential interest rate. This was essential, as private sector institutions would not have countenanced lending in the area.

The first phase of building began in 1982. It consists of 1,000 two-storey terraced houses containing two or three bedrooms. They are modestly sized by American standards (1,000–1,200 sq ft). They are constructed in a traditional style, faced with red brick. Standing in the middle of the formerly derelict land, these terraces, each with their own garden, make for a striking contrast. It is, almost, as if a portion of suburbia had suddenly been transported to the most unlikely location possible.

Much care was taken by the churches and Robbins to select a builder who could carry out the work efficiently. Further savings were made by obtaining professional services at low cost. The large scale of the plan and the use of only one standard design also enabled overhead costs to be spread more widely than would have been the case with a smaller scheme. The overall cost reductions were significant; similar units, built under one of the main federally subsidised programmes might cost up to $70,000, rather than the $43,500 they cost under the Nehemiah Plan. Applicants had to make a down payment of $5,000. This left $38,500 to be borrowed from the state funds at just under 10 per cent (all figures were current in 1986). The monthly mortgage charge was about $360.

When we visited the project in spring 1987 the revolving fund had reached $8m and 700 units had been completed, another 400 were being built and there were about 40 starts and 40 completions each month. Costs – and hence monthly mortgage charges – had risen to around $400, still a very moderate level by New York standards. The median income of the purchasers was $26,000 and 5,000 to 6,000 people had applied to buy the units that were still to be built. By late 1987 the project expected to have completed 1,100 units, making it the largest inner city home builder in the country. One problem was long delays in the city making cleared sites available which slowed down the rate of building considerably. Demand was far outstripping supply and the waiting list for houses had been closed for at least the next two years.

Professional fees for comparable projects usually amount to up to 30 per cent of total costs; in Nehemiah these have been cut to six per cent. Although the builder makes a profit, East Brooklyn Churches does not charge a developer's profit. The project is run by six paid staff but it also draws on the political negotiating skills of the local Industrial Areas Foundation organiser and volunteer church leaders. It is clear to us that this political organising, together with a technically competent plan for the housing and its financing, is essential to its success and to persuading or, where necessary, putting pressure on local politicians and officials to provide assistance. When a major problem had arisen from these sources the churches called a general assembly of their congregations to make a public protest. This, together with the support of the higher echelons of the church in the city, was something which politicians could not afford to ignore.

Unlike the next project to be discussed, those responsible for the

Nehemiah Plan do not believe that rehabilitation is the answer to meeting housing needs in their area. The remaining multi-storey buildings are severely deteriorated. They would have cost, on average, $80,000 a unit to rebuild. It would have required deep subsidies which are, anyway, unavailable, to make them affordable to local residents. Infill building and rehabilitation would also be very expensive. Therefore, they have opted for building low cost, low rise housing on completely cleared sites.

Of course, some subsidies are needed. As we have seen, apart from the free land it provides, the city directly contributes about $13,000 per unit in site costs and interest free loan, but will get some of this back if the houses are resold. It also exempts the units from property tax for 10 years.

However, in exchange, the area is beginning to revive and with it the long-term prospects for the local property tax base. The state finance, which costs two to three per cent below market rates, is provided by the sale of tax exempt bonds, so here the project receives the same indirect subsidy as many other middle-income projects, at the expense of federal – not state – revenues. In addition, homeowners can claim the normal tax allowances available to any US homeowner.

Even allowing for all these direct and indirect subsidies, the housing is far less deeply subsidised than previous federally supported attempts to extend low-income home ownership. The Nehemiah Plan has been able to provide affordable housing by carefully selecting a relatively cheap form of building and ensuring efficient production. A measure of the success of the programme was that, at the time of our visit, the resale prices of the first houses had already reached $65,000 to $70,000. However, few owners wished to sell as, even at these prices, better units could not be obtained on the private market elsewhere in the city.

Urban Homesteading Assistance Board and the Tenant Interim Lease Program

The Urban Homesteading Assistance Board is also involved in extending ownership to moderate and low-income households. It too operates in New York City, in areas where there are large numbers of deteriorating and abandoned private rental blocks. However, unlike the Nehemiah Plan, it links rehabilitation with the tenant takeover of multi-storey buildings and their co-operative ownership.

The Board, a non-profit organisation, was founded in 1974, by a group of community activists, to develop self-help solutions to the city's lack of low-income housing (we discuss its experience of self-help building in the next chapter). It obtained church, charitable and corporate funding and began by promoting urban homesteading. Later, it branched out into providing train-ing, technical and other services for tenants in self-help housing projects. By the mid-eighties it had 22 paid staff and an annual budget of $800,000, about two thirds of which came from the fees that the city paid for its services to the programme to be described here.

In the mid-seventies, due to a change in local laws, New York City began to own large numbers of deteriorating blocks of private rental housing which had been taken into possession because of property tax arrears (known as *in rem* properties, after the legal terminology indicating that they have been possessed in lieu of taxes). In 1978, faced with the prospect of becoming the city's largest slum landlord, city officials asked the board to help find a solution to this problem.

This resulted in the Tenant Interim Lease Program. The Assistance Board noted that, spontaneously, some tenants had been taking over manage-ment functions after their landlords had abandoned their properties. How-ever, this grass-roots self-help movement was not formally recognised by the city and the tenants had no legal title to the buildings.

According to Rebecca Reich, who works for the Urban Homesteading Assistance Board, it suggested that the tenants should be helped to take the buildings over and to carry through their renovation, using a combination of grants and loans. On completion, these would become tenant-owned co-operatives. She said, '*we argued that conversion to ownership would provide a much greater incentive for tenants to become involved in upgrad-ing the properties than if the city remained their landlord*'. From the city's point of view this option was attractive as it had no desire to take on additional, onerous and costly landlord functions.

Under the scheme, tenants who live in buildings which come into the city's possession have an option to enter the leasing programme. Certain condi-tions have to be met, buildings have to be at least 60 per cent occupied at the time of the city takeover and 60 per cent of the residents have to agree to the project. They then form a tenants association, elect officers and open a bank account. When these requirements are fulfilled they can join the programme.

The next stage – which lasts between two and three years – involves preparation for the formation of the tenant co-operative. The Assistance Board arranges training sessions which the tenants have to attend; it is paid by the city for these services. It provides training in all the necessary skills, such as book-keeping, maintenance and repair, how to organise a co-operative, hold meetings and take decisions. During this period city and board staff are assigned to the buildings. The Assistance Board provides technical advice, including helping the tenants to put together a budget for the project and assess the rent increases which will be necessary to make the co-operative economically viable. In addition, a repair plan is drawn up with items in prioritised order and the rules of the co-operative are established.

At the same time, the city makes a modest investment in basic repairs and replacements (such as roofing, heating, windows, rewiring, plumbing). On average, $5,000 a unit is spent over two to three years. The Board acts as an advocate for the tenants, pressing the city to do as much as possible in the period before responsibility is transferred to the tenants. Tenants pay rents to their association and the city is paid a nominal $1 annually per building. When the buildings come into the possession of the city all outstanding loan debts and back taxes are cancelled. Therefore, rents only have to cover the day to day running costs during the period but often some increases are needed, even at this first stage, to make ends meet.

The time taken to reach the stage of co-operative conversion is dependent on the strength of the tenants' commitment to the project and the emergence of capable leadership among them, but normally after two to three years the financial and organisational structure of the buildings are sufficiently sound for this to occur. According to Reich, '*the main thing the city is interested in is that the tenants know how to do book keeping*'. The city then sells the building to the co-operative. When the project started it was agreed the price should be $250 per unit, although, as we note below, there was subsequently a conflict over this agreement. The co-operative takes a special legal form only applicable to formerly city owned property. Some restrictions are attached to it, principally governing the income limits of the co-operative members. Each tenant buys a $250 share in the co-operative and leases their property from it.

At the time of our research, maintenance and operating expenses averaged $50–60 per room per month, average rents were around $250 per month which was very low by New York standards. However, even these low rents are not affordable by many households dependent on welfare benefits. So the city has used federal housing vouchers to help them meet the costs. But these are being cut, as is the Community Development Block Grant funding which the programme also uses. Most tenants belong to minority groups and are poor, many are single women with children on welfare benefits or elderly residents on low fixed incomes. The median tenant household income in 1985 was $15,000 per year, very low by local standards. Most properties are in black and Hispanic areas, although in a few locations there is potential for profitable resale of buildings, as gentrification has begun to encroach on them.

In theory, any profit which tenants make from sales has to be split 50:50 with the co-operatives but we were told that the co-operatives rarely get this money as sellers and buyers can collude to conceal any profits (although all new buyers have to be approved by the co-operatives). This raises a difficult issue of principle. The Program was created as an ownership programme for low-income households. If shareholders get windfall profits from the sale of their units the benefits will no longer pass to other low-income households. However, as Reich says, '*it's difficult to deny a poor person the money gains that other, middle class, homeowners can make*'.

The Board continues to provide some support after the co-operative has been formed. Usually, additional renovations are required (for which low interest block grant loans can be obtained from the city council) and there are other problems to be solved. The Board has founded a so-called mutual housing association, in this case a form of secondary co-operative, to provide services to the co-operatives. This arranges insurance on beneficial terms, purchases cheap bulk supplies, assists tenants in obtaining city loans for renovation and provides architectural and legal services. By 1987 about 200 buildings had been converted to co-operatives and another 400 were in progress. This was a major project involving about 40,000 people, making it one of the largest low-income housing programmes then operating in the USA.

However, there are some limits on the size and functioning of the Program. The city owns about 12,000 buildings which have been taken into possession for tax arrears. Most are vacant and will probably be beyond saving before anything can be done about them. However, about 4,000 buildings are still occupied, so the 500 in the Tenant Interim Lease Program only represent a minority of this stock. Of the remaining 3,500, most are managed directly by the city and about 300 by various community groups. Very few of these are being converted to co-operatives and, as the city continues to foreclose on properties, the size of its management problem is not being reduced.

Another problem concerns the high levels of property taxes paid by many of the buildings. The city is able to reduce assessments but only when renovation is carried out. In 1987 the position of some buildings worsened as a result of tax reassessments which the Assistance Board was trying to get reduced. In addition, there was conflict over the price at which the city sold the units to the tenants. Recently, some buildings near a new convention centre had come up for sale. This was an area which was likely to see rising property values due to its location. So the city had broken the rule that units should be sold for $250 and tried to charge $9,000. The tenants had protested and, according to Rebecca Reich, '*it became a huge political battle*'. In the end, the city agreed to stick to the original sale terms but enforced an agreement to share any resale profits equally between itself, the tenant and the co-operative.

In general, despite its support for the Program, the city is looking, where possible, to sell its properties in more promising areas to private buyers for higher profits. This undermines the extension of the co-operative conversion programme. Also, wherever possible, the city empties the more deteriorated buildings and closes them down permanently. This reduces the potential housing stock which can be renovated. It is also difficult to obtain loans for renovation as most buildings are in areas where private institutions refuse to lend.

In some cases, the tenants can finance work out of their accumulated reserves (as the co-operatives are not tax exempt this also means that they avoid building up a tax liability). But they often have to rely on the cheap loans financed by city block grant money and in 1987 the federal government had cut this by a quarter.

The Manna Project

A successful but much smaller scale project to expand lower-income home ownership is Manna, in Washington DC, which provides low cost, rehabilitated housing for purchase by households working in low paid jobs. It is a non-profit organisation which had been started in the early 1980s by a church-based organisation called 'For the Love of Children'. It particularly aims to provide housing for people who are trying to get re-established after living in the city's homeless persons' shelters and mothers who have had their children taken into care and cannot get them back due to a lack of housing. Originally, the financing for Manna had come through a form of shared equity, with high-income partners participating for the tax benefits, but, later, city and private funding has been mainly used.

Manna obtains cheap, but basically sound, housing in the poorer areas of the city and renovates it to minimal standards, using volunteer labour and its own paid – but socially committed – building force which does the work for much less than it can earn in the private sector. In these ways, renovation costs are reduced by 20 to 30 per cent. By the time of the research the organisation had renovated about 40 units, all for sale. Now other groups are coming to Manna wishing to employ its expertise. Manna is an unusually comprehensive organisation with an in-house building and design team and sales organisation.

The units are affordable by those '*on the low side of moderate income*', according to Johann Zimmerman, a worker with the project who spoke to us. In 1987, mortgage payments averaged $400 to $500 per month, about the same price as a low to moderate cost rental unit (Washington has a very expensive housing market with much pressure on the low-income housing stock in some areas due to gentrification). The acquired properties are very cheap, even as low as $5,000 to $10,000 per unit. Some have been empty for years, others are donated as tax write-offs by individuals. But they almost always need major renovation and this costs around $25,000 to $30,000. The work is kept as simple as possible but is done to a better standard than comparable units renovated by the private sector.

We visited one project, located in a somewhat dilapidated, but still functioning, inner area of the city. The building consisted of a three storey terraced house, built around the turn of the century. The property was structurally sound but had required a lot of work, redividing the internal spaces, installing modern heating and lighting, insulation and so on. We were shown round by one of the Manna building force whose strong commitment to the social objectives of the project was clear.

Most buyers work in low paid service occupations, most have in the past been dependent on welfare benefits. Manna provides considerable support and counselling, helping households to manage their finances so they can afford to buy. The buyers are eligible for the city's House Purchase Assistance Plan which supplies interest free loans of $16,000, provided that their incomes are no more than 80 per cent of the area median. These loans are combined with a first mortgage from private lenders at normal interest rates. The buyers also have to pay a five per cent deposit. Instead of the commercial first mortgage some buyers also qualify for cheaper loans from the city council which it raises by the sale of tax free housing bonds. This reduced the interest rate by two to three per cent, to about 8.5 per cent in early 1987. Manna also has a low interest, revolving loan fund contributed by local financial institutions, churches and wealthy individuals. This provides construction period finance; in some cases, the city government also makes no interest construction loans. In 1987 there was about $100,000 in this fund, most of it borrowed for between one and five years at low (one to five per cent) interest rates. In addition, the organisation has received some money from a commercial developer by a form of 'planning gain' which was negotiated by the local authority.

Buyers are referred to Manna by welfare organisations and the city housing department, or they learn of the programme by word of mouth. Considerable care is taken to assess applicants' ability to meet all home ownership costs: by 1987 there had been no mortgage defaults. All purchasers are first time buyers. Apart from having the necessary deposit, usually $2,000 to $3,000, buyers have to have incomes in the $15,000 to $25,000 range. In about half the cases there are two earners in the household. The house prices are normally around $55,000 – about 20 per cent below the market price for comparable units. Buyers benefit from a five-year property tax exemption, worth about $900 a year on the average unit.

There are no controls on resale but the local government loans must be repaid when this occurs. As with the Tenant Interim Lease Program, Johann

Zimmerman told us, '*Manna feels that it is hard to justify resale controls when better off homeowners are able to make capital gains*'. Apart from donations, Manna is mainly financed by the modest fees which it charges for its work, which average under $5,000 per unit. However, as its activities have developed (it is increasingly involved in lobbying the city over housing policies and offering help to other organisations), it is becoming more difficult to keep going on developers' fees alone.

The Oliemolens Project

As we mentioned earlier, innovatory developments such as Manna, Tenant Interim Lease and the Nehemiah Plan are less common in West Germany and the Netherlands, although we have already discussed the Rotterdam scheme for 'social' home ownership in chapter two. However, there is a novel project to help low-income owners to improve their properties at Enschede in the Netherlands. Buurtbeheer Oliemolens (Oliemolens Neighbourhood Management) involves an area of housing built around the turn of the century for workers in the town's textile industry. It consists of a wide variety of mainly semi-detached properties. In most cases, the workers had built the houses themselves. They are fairly large, narrow and deep units (a ground plan of five metres by nine metres is typical) and they have large gardens.

The problem faced by the low-income workers of these properties (many are foreign workers in poorly paid employment) is that major structural repairs are needed which their owners cannot easily afford. Government subsidies for private sector housing are available but these consist of many different schemes, are rather complicated and are not always attractive to low-income homeowners.

So the government agreed to an experiment to see whether effective means could be found to merge all these types of improvement and modernisation subsidies and redirect them to use for basic structural repairs. In this way, costs would be kept to a level which the occupants could afford. The programme also tries to carry out the work intensively in one area at a time. Normally, home owners' improvement work is done on an individual basis, which has little overall impact on the localities in which it occurs.

At the time of our research in 1987, average improvement costs were about 15,000 guilders per house and these were fully subsidised. The works usually consisted of replacing roof tiles, doors and windows and repairing walls. The owners contributed some money for additional items such as roof insulation. Between 30 and 50 houses were repaired at a time to obtain economies of scale, saving about 25 per cent in costs.

An association of homeowners has been formed in the neighbourhood with a small group of paid staff to organise the building work (their salaries are paid by the government's Experimental Housing Foundation, see chapter seven for a description of this organisation). The paid professionals have formed a separate office to organise the improvement works but the owners' association decides, in consultation with the paid staff, just how the work will be carried out. This form of organisation allows the homeowners to act as the clients for the work and the paid staff as their developer/ architects.

At the same time, the owners do not have to organise the work and can rely on the staff to provide the expertise that they lack. More recently, the staff have concentrated on advice work, leaving the provision of these professional development services to outside, hired agencies. This is regarded as more time efficient.

A continuing maintenance fund has been established for the houses. Homeowners contribute an annual fee and they hope to employ permanent maintenance staff at lower costs than if each owner made separate arrangements. But a minimum number of 100 owners have to join the scheme if it is to be feasible – with 200 members it can be financially self-supporting.

Oliemolens is an attempt to develop a limited degree of collective organisation among low-income homeowners (although there are also some private rental properties in the scheme). Elsewhere in the Netherlands, such owners face great difficulties in keeping their houses in good repair, given their low incomes and a subsidy scheme which is mainly intended to encourage modernisation and which assumes that homeowners are able to maintain their houses in good repair.

Some aspects of the scheme are reminiscent of British developments, such as care and repair, but the history of the scheme also illustrates some of the limits of this form of collective organisation. For example, there was resistance to the original aim of distributing subsidies according to the income levels of the owners. And an attempt to introduce resale controls failed. Again, the argument was – why should lower-income owners be unable to make the capital gains that the better off enjoyed? Finally, an attempt to lower the costs of the work by self-building was abandoned. It did not save greatly on costs and there were thought to be risks to the health and safety of the owners. (We discuss self-help at greater length in the next chapter.)

Discussion

The Nehemiah project has received a great deal of publicity in the USA because it is on a large scale, is operating in one of the most devastated inner city areas which has been written off as a hopeless case, and is apparently successful. In 1986 there was an unsuccessful campaign for a federal national demonstration programme and a bill was introduced into Congress to provide up to $150m in second mortgages similar to those provided by New York City. On a more modest basis, Manna is also under pressure to extend its operations and the Local Initiatives Support Corporation offered it financial support for this purpose.

However, in both cases there are serious doubts about whether and how such innovations can be expanded and transferred to other sites. This is, of course, a general matter of concern for this study too. In the case of Nehemiah, the federal Department of Housing and Urban Development argued, in opposition to the Congressional proposal, that the conditions in New York City were very special and unlikely to be found in many other locations. In particular, few cities had as much abandoned property and as many vacant lots as New York. Nor did many localities have such a strong community-based and politically effective organisation as that developed by the Brooklyn Churches.

While the federal government probably had ulterior motives in making these points (it did not want any new housing subsidies) the second point, in particular, seems important. Nehemiah is only possible because it grew out of an effective grassroots-based organisation which has strong links to politically powerful church leaders. Note too, that Nehemiah is not just a housing project, it is one aspect of a much wider attempt to revitalise the locality. Simply building the houses and doing no more would almost certainly result in failure.

For Manna an expansion of its operations presents somewhat different problems. The organisation originally intended to remain on a small scale, working intensively with its customers and as a closely knit team of socially committed workers. It also wished to be self-sufficient, funding itself from the development fees which it charged. Johann Zimmerman told us that the project workers were worried that many of these features will be lost if it becomes a larger and more bureaucratic organisation. Administrative and other costs not directly related to its development operations would grow, as it increasingly became involved in wider advisory and lobbying functions. It would have to divert effort to fund raising and the objective of self-sufficiency would be lost. It would probably also have to employ builders on a normal rather than 'socially committed' basis, as its current building force is willing to work for lower than average wages because of Manna's collective style of work and the lack of bureaucratic and remote management.

These two cases make us question how possible it is to replicate schemes from one area to another and what costs are incurred by the move from small to larger scale operations. Of course, these are matters of concern not just for innovations relating to lower-income home ownership. However, there are some more specific points relating to such projects as well;

▶ The question of whether housing, built or rehabilitated for lower-income home buyers, should be allowed to be resold on the open market and whether its sellers should keep any capital gains. If this is allowed, it is extremely difficult to build up a permanent stock of low-income housing. And it raises the question whether capital gains which have been created by public and collective effort should be privately appropriated. (Although it is hard to justify a ban on this in countries like Britain and the three nations discussed in this book, where private buyers are anyway massively subsidised by tax rebates and other assistance).

On the other hand, precisely because other better off households are able to benefit in this way, why should those on lower incomes lose out? In practice, it often seems difficult to enforce resale conditions, as in the case of the Tenant Interim Lease units. And the Oliemolens project discovered that its low-income owners would have been reluctant to become involved in the scheme if resale restrictions had been imposed. Every project discussed in this chapter has considered the issue. For various reasons, most have not chosen to try to retain the units for long-term occupation by lower-income households (But this experience contrasts with that of the Rotterdam 'social' home ownership project, discussed in chapter two).

▶ All the projects discussed here, with the exception of Oliemolens, use fewer direct housing subsidies than most previous attempts to foster lower-income home ownership. In this sense, they are interesting adaptions to contemporary circumstances, in which such subsidies have become much less available than they were a few years ago. At the same time, they are managing to provide new and improved housing for households who could not have bought without their help.

But the availability of substantial *indirect* subsidies remains crucial to their success. Cheap finance from the sale of tax subsidised housing bonds is an important element in all the American projects. Other forms of indirect subsidy include land at nominal prices, housing acquired at below market prices and property tax remissions. On any strict accounting basis the subsidies for these units may not really be much less than the more heavily directly subsidised programmes which they are trying to replace.

However, there is another more pragmatic way of looking at this issue. It is simply that such direct subsidies are not available so the organisations involved have to make use of whatever resources can be mobilised. The projects discussed here show what can sometimes be achieved by following this strategy.

▶ The other key element in achieving affordable housing is to reduce building costs. None of the projects discussed in this chapter involve any cost saving technology of the sort which – in the 1960s, in particular – was thought to be the answer to cheaper housing but which failed in practice. Instead, cost reductions are obtained by improvements in the existing methods and organisation of development.

First, there is an emphasis on building and improving the housing to standards which are set by two main considerations: minimally acceptable levels of space, amenity and structural soundness; and affordability. In the two European countries such standards are now similar to those adopted in Britain. However, in the USA, where such standards are considerably higher and tend to be set by the requirements and incomes of much better off households, considerable savings result from this approach.

A second source of significant cost-saving relates to developers' fees, building labour costs and professional fees. To varying degrees and in varying ways, all the projects make such savings. Perhaps the most comprehensive cost savings are achieved by Manna which only charges a cost-covering developer's fee and also employs its own in-house team of builders and professionals which is paid far less than its private sector equivalents. The Urban Homesteading Assistance Board's project development services are supplied on a cost-covering non-profit basis to the co-operatives and the Oliemolens project is paid for by an experimental housing grant. Nehemiah employs professionals cheaply and also manages to obtain reduced charges from the outside design, legal and other services which it requires.

Finally, there are cost savings by economies of scale. Thus, it is argued that the Nehemiah project should be large-scale to spread development overheads. The Urban Homesteading Assistance Board has set up a mutual housing association which provides cheap bulk purchase and non-profit services to the co-operatives and the Oliemolens project enables the houses of individual owners to be repaired at considerably lower costs than if each owner made separate arrangements for the work.

6. Self-help in Design and Construction

W e have already discussed one form of self-help in housing – tenant management – in chapter three and in relation to the Tenant Interim Lease programme work in the last chapter. We have also referred, in passing, to the use of self-help or 'sweat equity' as a way of minimising the cost of housing for low-income households. In many countries there is a tradition of self-help building, normally of single family houses in rural areas. In West Germany, this has been on a fairly large-scale but it has been less common in the USA, Britain and in the Netherlands (although one should not overlook the substantial amount of self-help building by owner-occupiers – and even some tenants – in carrying out DIY improvements).

A good deal of this self-building has been carried out by households with considerable resources. Such households are involved in self-building because it will enable them to obtain better housing than they could afford on the open market or a type of housing, or of living arrangements, which they prefer. However, in this chapter we focus on the contribution that self-building and design might be able to make to reducing the housing costs of lower-income households as well as enabling them to obtain housing which is suitable for their particular needs. We shall particularly concentrate on collective forms of self-help building. In practice, most of these schemes concern existing buildings because new building is too costly. Such self-help initiatives are often combined with self-management of the completed housing. However, we first examine a few of the relatively small number of new self-help schemes and a related design method.

'Open building'

Open bouwen – open building – is not in itself an example of self-building, only of self-design. We have chosen to discuss it because it offers potential opportunities for incorporating an element of self-building in the construction of new housing and possibly also in the conversion or rehabilitation of existing buildings.

Open building is an approach to design and building first developed by architectural theorists who were concerned to increase the role of the occupants of new housing in its design. Cost saving was not a central concern. It involves a method of modular building and design which separates the construction of housing into two parts, the shell and the infill. The shell consists of all the structural elements of the building – foundations, floor, walls, roof, plus the main service outlets. The infill refers to the rest of the unit, partition walls, kitchen and bathroom fixtures and fittings and so on. This separation allows great flexibility in the pattern of internal arrangements and in the level of facilities provided, subject to some basic constraints relating to the modular form and to the location of water, gas and electricity inlets.

According to the architects who developed open building, it would have two advantages. First, when the buildings are constructed each new occupant can influence the internal design and layout of the unit. They saw the lack of any real consumer input to housing design as one of the main weaknesses of mass twentieth century housing and wanted to reduce the architect's power to impose his or her own solutions because these were often disliked by the consumer. In addition, within limits, consumers would have more freedom to decide just how much they would spend on the internal design and facilities. A second advantage of open building was that, when the unit was vacated, it could easily be re-adapted to the needs of the new occupants. It had taken some years to develop these ideas from theory into practice. This required the manufacture of modularised building components, kitchens and bathrooms, plumbing elements and so on. But by the late 1970s several projects were being constructed in the Netherlands (and a pioneering one in Britain by the Greater London Council – the Adelaide Road Estate in Camden).

We examined the role which open building had played in the development of a 152 unit development of social housing. It is located in the Keyenburg District of Zuidwijk, a garden city outside Rotterdam. Most the land had been developed for social and other housing in the 1950s. These properties surround the project on three sides – most buildings are four storeys high – but there is a lot of open space and a good environment. The project was completed in 1984 and consists of one and two person units, built under a special subsidy scheme for such dwellings. The estate consists of a series of low rise, three and five storey blocks, built with large concrete panels. Each unit has a balcony and overlooks the semi-private garden court around which they are grouped. Externally, they look just like any conventionally built housing constructed with concrete panel technology.

The tenants were selected when the shell of the building was being completed. Given that the housing was produced under the social housing subsidy rules, there was an upper limit to what could be spent on the infill. One of the architects who designed the building and worked with the tenants on its completion told us that tenants were supplied with written and illustrated material on available facilities, the constraints on dividing up the internal space and the costs of each element of the infill. There was a large shed with light movable partitions and furniture mock-ups in which they could try out their ideas. These ideas were discussed with the architects and, using a computer programme, the costs of the infill and therefore, the rent was calculated. If this was too high the design could be adjusted and the rent recalculated very quickly.

There were various complications, some concerned the constraints imposed by local building regulations, the rules for social housing construction and cost limits. Others related to the problems which the prospective tenants had in assimilating all the information provided by the architects. However, the tenants were said to be generally highly satisfied by the completed units and there was approximately a five per cent saving on building costs (excluding costs which arose because new procedures, computer programmes and other matters had to be developed for the first time).

The Keyenburg architects had collected a number of case studies, showing how tenants had reacted to the opportunity to design their own homes, its benefits and its costs. One couple, in their sixties and not in good health, had chosen to situate their living room in a particular location to maximise their privacy. However, it meant that the sun never entered the room, so they had taken to sitting in the bedroom on fine days. They also regretted that this design necessitated a long passageway. They now realised that this was lost space which could have been better used to increase the size of the living room. They were highly satisfied with the participation process, nonetheless. They had dropped all cupboards from the design, they already had some and their omission enabled the rent to be lowered. They also economised on electricity points in return for a lower rent.

A second inhabitant was an artist by profession. He particularly liked the project because he had been able to design his unit to suit his working requirements. These were for a large studio, located on the side of the building where it would receive maximum light. Apart from this, he had opted for as open a layout as possible, with only the bathroom and kitchen enclosed by partition walls. His sitting/sleeping area was located in the middle of the unit and the dining area near the front door, only being separated from it by a low partition. Because the infill was minimal, he paid the lowest possible rent.

From the point of view of potential cost saving, it seemed promising that open building could enable occupants to reduce costs by initially choosing a very basic layout and facilities, possibly adding to them later. These costs could be reduced even further if the occupants themselves assembled, installed – and in some cases – made the infill. The availability of modular 'off the shelf' building components, fixtures and fittings (a product of the DIY revolution) made this a relatively easy task. Now, even plumbing and wiring is possible by this means.

However, these cost saving possibilities had not really been exploited in the various Dutch projects. One reason was that most of these experiments had involved social rented housing. In most cases, the subsidy scheme for this housing was inflexible and did not allow lower building costs to be reflected in lower rents; at best, cost saving on one aspect of a scheme could be used to support additional costs in other parts of the project. In this respect, Keyenburg, which used a special subsidy scheme that did enable some rent reductions to be achieved, was an exception. (In 1988, after our research was completed, a new subsidy scheme did provide some more flexibility but the housing allowance regulations continued to operate in a way which discouraged cost saving.) However, a new project was just being started by a housing association which was going to allow some degree of self-building of the infill by the tenants. A further concern in the social sector was that, with the Dutch government trying to reduce building standards and costs, open building might simply be taken up as a useful way of achieving this, with minimal infill provision becoming the norm and tenants having to pay extra rent for anything above this level.

Interestingly, several of the major Dutch house builders have taken up open building and are developing systems for the production of rental and owner-occupied housing. Some of these firms are promoting a sort of shared equity, where the occupants rent the shell and buy the infill. One general problem about schemes which treat infill and shell separately concerns their financing. It has been suggested that costs could be reduced by amortising the loan for the shell over a period closer to its economic life, say 75 years. However, this cost saving would almost certainly be lost by the corresponding need to repay the cost of the less durable infill over a much shorter period, say 10 to 15 years. A loan period of about 25 years for the infill would be required if significant cost saving was to occur but this seems unrealistic. In any event, financial institutions are not very keen to split the financing in this way.

There have also been studies of how to apply the open building principles to rehabilitation with the structure of the existing building acting as the shell. The method seems feasible, although there are some problems relating to modular co-ordination. In fact, the architects responsible for the project which we visited had prepared plans for the rehabilitation of a 200 unit development which had been built in the 1950s and the scheme was waiting for official approval.

In practice, so far the structure/infill separation seems mainly to have involved a separation in who is being consulted at different stages in the design. Management and financing have remained in the hands of the housing associations. The open building architects see their role rather narrowly; it is to provide the technical tools for organising flexible space. They are not concerned, for example, with the financing of the projects or their management. Their clients are the housing associations whose main concern is to own a stock which can be flexibly adapted to changing needs. Given the Dutch subsidy scheme, the linking of open building to self-help seems more feasible in owner-occupied housing.

Self-building in Rotterdam

At the time of our research four self-build projects for lower-income households had been completed in Rotterdam, about 120 newly built units in all. Two of these projects had been promoted by the department of the local authority which controlled its land holdings. The self-builders had been recruited by advertisements – there had been a far greater number of applicants than the number of available building plots. The work was co-ordinated by an architect and involved a mixture of subcontracting and self-help labour. Savings amounted to about 30,000 guilders per unit. Two thirds of this was due to reduced building costs and one third to savings in development costs. This was a cost saving of about 25 per cent.

The houses took about nine months to complete. An evaluation study carried out by the Technical University at Delft found that most self-builders were positive about the experience. More than three quarters of them said that they would do it again. However, according to an architect who had been involved with the project, 'there was much enthusiasm but overall the experience was considered very difficult'.

The self-builders felt that too much responsibility was left in their hands, although 'they liked being an international tourist attraction' (as municipal officials and others took parties of visitors to the site!). There were several problems. First, the self-builders were in a weak position to bargain with materials suppliers. They could not threaten to go elsewhere for the next contract if they got bad service, unlike commercial and public sector builders. Second, there were problems of timing. Building materials had often not arrived at the time when the builders were available to do the work. Third, self-building was very time consuming. It was expected that partici-pants would have to spend three evenings a week and Saturdays on the project and that it would take six months to complete. In practice, they had to spend four evenings and the whole weekend building and the project took nine months.

These projects had been so time consuming because the participants had built the complete houses. In later projects, construction of the shell has been left to contractors. Using modern machinery and prefabrication, it takes a contractor no more than a few days to do what it had taken the self-builders six months to complete. Although the contractors have to be paid, the time taken to self-build the shell is also costly for the participants, not only in terms of stress and so on, but financially as they have to meet their existing housing costs during this time. So the self-building effort later became focused on the design stage plus finishing. Savings amounted to about 10,000 guilders per unit.

There was no formal training for the self-builders, although they were given some written material and there was a site supervisor who assisted them and inspected finished work. Learning this way seemed to be more effective than formal instruction but, in any event, according to the architect we interviewed, the type of self-build work being done on the later houses did not need much training. *'It is designed for DIY and only a few tricks have to be learnt'*. Similar projects are underway in several other Dutch cities and, interestingly, some commercial house builders are beginning to develop sites where houses can be bought either fully finished or in shell form with the completion work left to the purchaser.

The Chorweiler estate – Cologne

With the decline of social house building in West Germany the possibilities for collective self-building have begun to be explored by progressive architects and planners. Traditionally, self-building has been common in West Germany. However, it has been individually organised and been carried out by more affluent households. It has been estimated that in such projects, on average, some 2,000 hours are spent on building work by the future owners of the property, their families and friends. Whereas, it has been estimated that around 1,100 hours is the most one person with a full time job (necessary for a mortgage loan) can devote to building in a year. Even this requires a daunting effort, for example, four hours every weekday evening, a day at the weekend and four weeks of annual holiday.

One project involved an area of land on Chorweiler, a 1960s built peripheral social housing estate to the north of Cologne. The site had been intended for high rise building but this never materialised. In 1983, three firms of architects were invited to develop a new plan for the site. It was decided that family houses would be built for workers, most from the nearby

Ford plant, using self-help methods. This scheme was promoted by the local authority which owned the land and the trade unions were involved in the selection of the self-builders.

The land was subdivided by the local authority and sold off in 33 plots. There were three teams of self-builders, each responsible for 11 houses. The Kölner Planwerkstatt was one of the three groups of architect planners involved in the project. It had already been involved in a number of smaller self-built projects carried out by groups of skilled manual workers, including guest workers. Two of the building teams had the basic structures of the houses erected by a contractor but the Planwerkstatt group did all the work itself.

Some of the group had building skills but not the majority. Each member was obliged to spend 70 hours a month on the work; the group elected one of their number to monitor this. The houses were all built in a year, working in the evenings, at weekends and in holidays. 50,000 DM was saved on each unit, which amounted to about a third of the building costs (excluding land costs). The total cost per unit was about 225,000 DM, very cheap by German standards. The owners also received subsidised loans under the general scheme for subsidised (social) homeowner building.

Most of the savings came from the self-building of the shell. Less could be saved on the finishing costs as there was a high proportion of manufactured components which had to be bought in (for example, window frames, kitchen and bathroom fitments and so on). However, most self-build projects, unlike this one in Cologne, tend to concentrate on finishing work. Cost savings may also be made by reducing the variety of plans used, as this saves on architects' fees. Interestingly, however, the Chorweiler self-builders were often keen to spend some additional money to make the external appearance of their houses look different from those of others in the scheme.

Urban Homesteading Assistance Board – sweat equity projects

In chapter five we discussed the Urban Homesteading Assistance Board's work in assisting the tenant takeover of landlord abandoned buildings. But, as we noted, when this organisation began in the early 1970s its main concern was to assist the development of low-income urban homesteading in New York City. This programme was still continuing at the time of our research. It has given the organisation a great deal of experience concerning the opportunities and problems presented by self-help building, or 'sweat equity' to use the American term.

From the late 1960s there had been some interest in the USA in the potential savings to be gained from sweat equity projects. In 1976 the federal government funded a national demonstration programme of urban home-steading in apartment blocks which the Assistance Board co-ordinated and supervised. This programme combined various forms of housing subsidies, tax reliefs and job training funds. It was carried out over five years in six cities. In New York 12 buildings with over 100 units were involved. Various problems arose. The job training programmes were not very appropriate to the practical needs of housing production and it proved difficult to obtain the right sort of financial arrangements. One important problem was the limited extent to which self-help building could substitute for the work of professional builders. In response to this the assistance board developed a 'Sweat-Contractor-Sweat' plan, whereby self-help was used for initial demolition and clearance work and for finishing, while the basic structural works were carried out by contractors.

The board's general conclusions concerning sweat equity are interesting. It has proved to be neither quick nor easy, nor, by conventional standards, particularly efficient. It is probably not the best method of low cost housing production. If the main objective is to expand supply, conventional methods can produce housing more quickly and more efficiently. In fact, the New York projects saved around 15 to 20 per cent of the building costs. But self-building has several payoffs. Among these are the job training opportunities provided, the encouragement of co-operative ownership, affordability for low-income households and, more generally, the positive impact that the projects have on the declining areas in which they are mainly located.

Self-help improvement in West Berlin

By the time of our research there were many projects in West Germany which were using self-help to improve housing for lower-income house-holds. The organisations we shall now discuss, based in Berlin and Han-nover, are just two among many who have been recognised as developers under the German urban renewal act. They are non-profit institutions which aim to support lower-income housing improvement. Because of the low incomes this usually involves self-help. A key contribution of such organisa-tions is the help which they give the self-builders in dealing with excessively bureaucratic government, financial and housing institutions and practices.

The first projects which we discuss involve an organisation called the Sozialpadagogiches Institut, 'The Social Education Institute' which operates in West Berlin. Volker von Tiedemann, an Institute worker, told us that it is a non-profit welfare organisation whose housing work is funded by the city government. It aims to combine the creation of housing with work and education. Its projects involve assisting groups of low-income, disadvan-taged, inner city tenants or squatters, living in buildings which have been bought from private owners by the council and which are located in urban renewal areas.

Most housing rehabilitation in these areas is carried out by urban renewal companies. The cost of work is high so the rents are not affordable by the original residents who are displaced. The conflict over this issue was one of the factors which led to large scale squatting in Berlin. The Institute became involved because of its social work with unemployed youth, foreign workers and women's groups. For this reason, in the early 1980s, the city council asked it to mediate between the authorities and the squatter groups and to help the squatters develop low cost housing improvements.

These works are carried out under the provisions of the urban renewal act. To be recognised for assistance under this act, the groups have to contribute 15 to 20 per cent of the costs of the works in self-help and organise themselves into a formally constituted association or corporation. At first, the city owned properties are transferred to the Institute, later the tenants buy them. A subsidy scheme specially designed for self-help is used. Each building operation is described in detail and subsidised by a fixed amount. To operate this successfully requires much technical input from the supervising architects and a high input of self-help. Cost overruns result in higher housing costs. However, unanticipated savings mean lower costs.

Total improvement subsidies are limited to 800 DM per square metre. Total costs have to be kept to 1,000 DM per square metre. This is low by West Berlin standards. (In 1987 improvement costs were typically around 1,200 DM to 1,600 DM per square metre). The 200 DM gap between subsidies and total costs is met by 'sweat equity'. These rules limit what can be achieved. Nevertheless, most of the Institute buildings had originally been listed for demolition but with self-help they are being successfully brought up to an adequate basic standard while being retained for lower-income occupation. After the work is finished the tenants buy the buildings collectively. If necessary, they can do this over time by a form of rental purchase agreement. A variety of restrictions over the resale or disposal of the buildings remain in force for 15 years and ensure that they will continue to be available for lower-income households.

The tenant groups themselves usually act as the initiators of projects, approaching the Institute with requests for it to assist. Self-management and ownership put high demands on such groups. Helping to manage group dynamics appears to be an important part of the Institute's supporting role, especially at first. In time, however, the groups' self-confidence grows as they gain skills and knowledge about the building process.

In 1987, 1,000 units a year were being improved with the special subsidies in West Berlin, about 10 per cent of all housing renovation in the city. The city government was providing about 40 million DM a year for the programme. However, two thirds of this money was, in fact, going to associations of individual homeowners, not the tenant co-operatives described above. Such homeowners could, unlike the tenants, claim individual tax relief (although the tenants could convert their organisations into homeowner associations and then get the relief). In fact, a change was occurring in the nature of the scheme. Initially, as described, it was mainly for low-income tenants. Now, as Volker von Tiedemann told us, ' *such groups are becoming an exception, more middle class homeowners are using the scheme. With the gentrification of inner areas of the city and political changes in city government, subsidised self-help is increasingly becoming a middle class programme*'.

The Linden Self-help Co-operative – Hannover

This project involves a co-operative which was founded in 1982 to purchase and improve buildings in an urban renewal area called Linden. The aim, as in Berlin, is to preserve low cost housing for low-income residents who are usually displaced by urban renewal, using self-help in building and management.

In 1983 the Co-operative purchased its first two buildings, containing eight units, from the local authority. Further properties have since been acquired. These costs are met by a form of monthly rental payment by the occupants. Only residents of the locality who meet the income criteria for admission to social housing can become tenants. Each member has to buy a share in the co-op which costs 1,000 DM, but this can be – and usually is – contributed in kind, by self-help labour, rather than in cash. In addition, the Co-operative has some non-resident members who have supported its work by buying shares.

Rents after improvement are fixed at not more than 5.50 DM per square metre and are to remain at this level for 25 years. This rent covers the costs of acquisition, improvement and running costs. The cost of improvements for the first two buildings was 1,900 DM per square metre. Twenty per cent of this was provided by the Co-operative, the rest came from urban renewal funds; five per cent of the Co-operative's 20 per cent contribution was borrowed commercially, the other 15 per cent came from the share subscriptions and from self-help contributions. The building work was supervised by three local architects; much of their contribution was free of charge.

Although the urban renewal act allows 15 per cent of the costs to be contributed by self-help, this cannot be capitalised in the form of co-operative shares. In other words, the Co-operative cannot build up its equity stake in the projects through self-help. A second problem is that self-help contributions are valued by the authorities at 20 per cent less than equal work which is professionally carried out, so the amount of self-help labour which the tenants have to contribute, to meet their 15 per cent share of the improvement costs, is increased.

A more general problem, experienced by many self-builders elsewhere, is the impact on family life of self-building. Some households have even come close to breaking up under the stresses and strains of the work. This also places a heavy burden on the tenants' professional advisers who not only have to supervise the work, for which they earn a normal commercial fee, but carry out much unpaid work, including help with financial management, progress chasing and even amateur social work with the families. After such a stressful experience it is perhaps not surprising that the tenants have been unwilling to take over management responsibilities, as was originally planned when the buildings were completed.

Another problem was that many tenants moved out soon after completion, wishing to realise the capital which they had contributed by their labour. This has drained the Co-operative of capital resources as there are no controls to prevent it. The same problem has also arisen in a number of similar self-help improvement projects in Nuremburg which we investigated during the research (although these are not, in fact, co-operatives but 'associations of tenants').

Self-building and housing conversions in the Netherlands

One of the most extensive projects which included self-building had occurred in the Netherlands. This concerned the conversion of redundant public, commercial and industrial buildings by groups of self-builders. The programme was initiated by Landelijke Organisatie Belangengroepen Huisvesting, a government funded group which supported low-income housing initiatives (see chapter seven).

In the first instance the project involved a series of feasibility studies. Working with money provided by a government backed experimental housing foundation, (discussed in chapter seven) two architects employed by the low-income housing group issued a general call to groups which were trying to convert property for their own use as housing; 41 groups responded and the architects selected 23 for full feasibility studies.

Trevor James, one of the architects involved, explained that most of these groups were aiming to obtain standard social housing subsidies which were designed for the production of relatively expensive newly built units for one and two person households and many wanted to use some self-building to lower costs. So, unlike the open building project discussed earlier, these projects were actually trying to use self-help in social housing construction and to apply the subsidy system to shell/infill construction. Proposals to do this had been previously discussed in the Netherlands but had always been rejected by government.

Many of the groups consisted of young, low-income individuals and couples who had squatted the buildings which they now wished to convert. Others included a group which wanted to provide elderly peoples' housing and some youth workers who wanted to convert an old school for young persons' housing. Two groups were in competition – both were trying to get plans approved to convert an old orphanage in Haarlem. Several groups wanted to convert buildings to provide living and working spaces.

Throughout 1984 the two architects worked with the groups to examine the feasibility of their projects. First, each group set out how it wanted to live and what were the maximum shelter costs which it could afford. It was then possible to explore just how, if at all, these two sets of requirements could be met.

A great many difficulties needed to be overcome. In particular, the social housing regulations were quite inflexible in relation to the non-standard requirements of the groups, for example, the combination of living and working space. Self-help building, which many groups wanted to do in order to reduce costs, also created difficulties. The rent regulations for social housing prevented the full value of the savings made by self-building being reflected in lower rent levels. The two consultants argued that the groups should be able to choose the level of quality of the finished buildings. At the minimum, they should be able to pay a basic rent for a structurally sound and safe shell, with all the major services connected. The maximum quality level would be the same as the current standard for all social housing.

The groups wanted to be involved in managing the development process, aided by their professional advisers, as well as having some control over the process of allocating future vacancies, especially in group housing. Such ideas were not accepted by most housing associations and local authorities, although some had eventually realised that, where group housing was concerned, it was a mistake to impose new tenants without the involvement of existing residents.

At the end of the project, its results were presented to a conference of tenants' groups, local and central government representatives and one of the two national federations of housing associations (which had close links with the labour movement). According to James, *'there was a very negative response from NWR (National Federation of Housing Associations). They accused us of propagating the waste of housing association expertise because of our self-management recommendations. They ...felt threatened by the recommendations. The central government spokesman was also scathing about the quality recommendations and the suggestion for paid tenant advisors. He said that these proposals would have been OK in the sixties when there was more money but not now. But this makes no sense, our proposals would not cost a lot and might even save some money'*.

Despite this opposition, some projects have been built but they had to find ingenious ways round the constraints of the subsidy system or '*they have capitulated to its conditions*'. One project had been clever enough to use a special subsidy system only available for the restoration of historic buildings. This group wanted to live communally, not in separate units. However, the subsidy scheme required conventional housing to be created. The solution here was to show on the plans a number of 'fictive units'! Self-building has mainly involved the infill, not the shell, of the buildings. The amount of money that has had to be spent on the shells of these buildings has varied widely, from 30 to 70 per cent of the total building costs, so the scope for self-build savings has also varied a good deal.

The Woonwinkel project – Tilburg

In Tilburg, a small town in the south of the Netherlands, some younger households have formed an organisation called Woonwinkel ('housing workshop') to rehabilitate housing for groups that are not effectively catered for by existing forms of provision. These include households dependent on low wages or social security benefits. As the Woonwinkel project grows, it is envisaged that it will adopt a federal structure, with a separate co-operative in each building, a federation of the co-operatives with Woonwinkel acting as the development agency. At the time of our research it had renovated five houses. These all dated back to the late nineteenth and early twentieth centuries and ranged in size from a small, 'two up, two down' terrace house to some larger, now dilapidated but formerly middle class properties.

Members of the workshop explained to us that Woonwinkel does not initiate development. It is approached by groups who want to acquire a building and rehabilitate it for their own accommodation. The organisation works with these groups to develop their proposals, arranges the acquisition of buildings, and obtains financing. There are many problems to be resolved, including securing loans for people, many of whom have state benefits as their only source of income. Difficulties are also created by rehabilitation subsidy rules which make certain assumptions about 'normal' patterns of family living not applicable to group living.

The project began in 1983 with a loan from the government's Experimental Housing Foundation (see chapter seven) to buy the first building. Rehabilitation was carried out by the Woonwinkel staff, a supervising architect and the people who were to live in the building. This project having succeeded, the group was able to convince the local authority to provide mortgage guarantees for further projects.

In Holland, individual homeowners can obtain 100 per cent mortgage guarantees from the local authorities. This scheme is meant for individual houses, not the sort of collective building which this project involves. But, according to the workers we spoke to, '*we showed the councillors and the alderman of finance that they had less risk with our projects than with the normal guarantees*'. So the local authority has bent the rules and agreed to guarantee a loan of up to 35,000 guilders per person, depending on their level of income and ability to pay. However, the incomes of each group were pooled for the purpose of this calculation, so groups which included people on very low incomes, who would not normally have got this level of guarantee, were combined with those on higher incomes with a higher guarantee limit. The members of the co-operative also benefit from the fact that they are not legally regarded as tenants but as homeowners, so that they can obtain the normal homeowner tax reliefs.

The question of how housing payments are related to incomes is left to each individual building to decide. At the time of the research, a decision on whether those who left the properties could take any of the equity with them had yet to be made but it was likely that most of the equity would be retained by the federation. One reason for this was that, under Dutch unemployment benefit rules, unemployed homeowners would lose their income support if they built up equity in their houses. Also, if the federation retained the equity, its financial situation would be strengthened and hence its ability to form new co-operatives.

Much has been learnt while completing the first few buildings. The first house was in a very poor condition and had been bought very cheaply, for 18,000 guilders. Originally, the group intended to use a contractor for most of the basic work but builders were not keen to work with such a group and raised tender prices. So the group did the work itself with the advice and assistance of a retired builder. The cost of this project, which only housed two people, was too high. It amounted to 92,000 guilders plus the labour of the group (estimated value 18,000 guilders), but its market value was only about 80–90,000 guilders. The house was too small and dilapidated to make it an economic proposition – later properties have been larger and in better basic condition. Also, like many other Dutch projects, the Tilburg workshop had found that '*the subsidy rules are very restrictive, they inhibit flexibility. They also penalise self-building, we only get subsidy to cover part of the cost of materials, whereas if we had used a contractor it would have covered labour costs plus materials*'.

Discussion

In this chapter we have briefly reviewed a wide range of self-design and self-build projects in all three countries. These initiatives encounter many difficulties. The contribution of largely self-built projects to the expansion of affordable low-income housing is likely to remain modest, though it could expand beyond its current very limited application. However, there seems less reason why, especially with the development of techniques such as open building and new building components, there should not be a more extensive growth of housing consumers' involvement in the design of housing and the finishing work.

Although this may not contribute much to cost reduction it has other advantages, especially in relation to the production of housing which is better adapted to the specific needs of certain households. This is significant given the decline of the 'standard' household, leading to a mismatch between housing needs and the accommodation offered by mass housing, both in the private and in the social sectors.

Our more specific conclusions are:-

▶ Few projects manage to save more than 25 per cent in building costs and then only with a very great expenditure of time and effort by the self-builders. The savings on infill self-building, which is in most cases all that it is feasible to attempt, are normally around 10 per cent or less (but such self-building activity is far less time consuming; it amounted to about 250 hours, on average, in some of the Dutch projects)

▶ Self-builders, aided by adequate professional support and advice, achieve a standard of construction which seems to be quite adequate in most cases. Indeed, some projects feel that finishing work is done better by self-builders than by contractors.

▶ Virtually all the projects have serious difficulties in coping with the rules and regulations of housing systems which are set up to finance, subsidise and build 'normal' housing by public or commercial developers. In many cases, ingenious ways have to be found round these rules but this is often costly, time consuming and increases the groups' reliance on professional advice. In addition, there is often a good deal of hostility to the self-builders' efforts on the part of officials and private builders. If self-building is to be expanded these problems will need to be resolved. It is interesting to note that advocates of self-building in third world cities, notably John Turner, have also pointed to the problems which occur when self-building has to be 'fitted in' to systems which are not designed to accommodate it.

▶ While self-building is often a satisfying experience for many of the participants, it is also a time consuming and stressful activity which can place considerable strain on individuals and their families. To help deal with this, as well as the many technical and other difficulties, it seems essential that professional support be available for self-builders, especially when they have limited financial and other resources.

▶ The interest of building companies, financial institutions and housing professionals in methods of providing more flexible systems of housing provision which are adaptable to changing needs should be mentioned. Many of the schemes, which we have described, were developed to provide low cost housing for disadvantaged groups but competition between such groups and better off households has been growing. As a result, house prices in some inner urban areas have been rising.

▶ Finally, the current pattern of tax subsidies for home ownership also tends to aid the better off. Such trends put low-income groups at a major disadvantage and may, as we saw in the Berlin case, mean that self-help schemes are not serving those for whom they were originally intended.

7. Organisations Supporting Housing Innovation

O ne of the key features of the innovative housing projects described in this book is the crucial role played by what might be described as 'enabling organisations'. In the United States, for example, we saw how the Local Initiatives Support Corporation and the Enterprise Foundation operate to channel private sector funding to low-income housing and how the Neighbourhood Reinvestment Corporation and the Urban Homesteading Assistance Board aid the development of various forms of co-operative and self-built housing. More generally, many projects require considerable assistance from professional advisers if they are to succeed.

So a wide range of organisational and professional support is essential if housing innovations are to develop. However, in housing systems which are dominated by long established institutions, procedures and political and professional attitudes, such support is not always available.

In this chapter we focus on several organisations which, apart from aiding specific projects, also have a more general concern with promoting, evaluating and disseminating information about housing innovations.

Community Information Exchange

Most of the types of housing innovations that we have been discussing in this book involve small-scale, locally-based projects. Large-scale, national changes in housing policies and markets often get a good deal of publicity in the media as well as more considered and detailed analysis in the specialist housing periodicals and in academic studies. But it is very difficult to obtain an overview of the mass of localised developments that are now occurring. This lack of information inhibits the diffusion of knowledge about new developments in housing, with several important consequences. It hinders the growth of support networks linking together similarly constituted projects. And it may mean that new projects will not be able to benefit from the experience of other developments.

All too often, we suspect, projects are having to 'reinvent the wheel', learning the hard way, by trial and error, when a greater acquaintance with the history of parallel projects elsewhere would enable them to avoid some aspects of this costly process. Given the limited resources available for housing innovation, it is important that there should be a cumulative growth of information and intelligence rather than a wasteful duplication of effort.

It is not surprising that this problem has been particularly evident in the USA. With its vast size, its wide range of local housing policies and markets, and the high level of locally-based housing activism, there is a clear need for a readily accessible, central source of intelligence about new developments. The Community Information Exchange was established in 1983 to fill this gap. The Exchange was initially sponsored by the National Urban Coalition, one of the best known organisations which act as a lobby group on behalf of the urban poor. Later, it became a separate non-profit organisation, supported by a charitable foundation and some income from users and other fees. It is based in Washington DC and employs eight staff, six of whom work on its information exchange. In 1987 it had an annual budget of $260,000.

Alice Shabecoff, the Exchange's director, describes it as, 'a one-stop center for the resources, information, guidance and referrals needed to plan, finance, and develop community revitalisation projects'. She explained to us that its central element is a computerised data base which contains detailed information about community-based economic development and housing projects (the closest equivalents in Britain, but only dealing with economic development, are the Planning Exchange in Scotland and the Centre for Employment Initiatives in England). The Exchange's staff have two main roles, to collect the information on these projects and to assist and guide those who wish to access it. The staff has various specialisms, such as fund raising, community organising, grants and contracts administration, housing development, technical assistance and non-profit management.

The Exchange uses specially developed software which enables it to present the information it collects in a uniform way and allows users, via a system of keywords, to carry out rapid searches of the data base. These searches can be carried out by the Exchange staff or by directly accessing the computer using a modem. Each entry consists of up to two or three pages of information. This includes basic details, location, type of project, types of needs addressed and the distinguishing characteristics of the project (the last two consisting of lists of key words).

In addition, there is data on project costs and capital requirements, the socio-economic and ethnic composition of the areas in which the projects are located and a contact name and address. There is also a brief (500 –1,000 word) description and analysis of the project, its history, progress and an account of the successes and failures which have been experienced.

The Information Exchange has also developed a range of supplementary resources. It has compiled a full list of funding agencies, covering central, state and local sources as well as foundations, church-based funds and so on. There is also a nationwide directory of technical advisors, a bibliographical data base, a library of research reports and practical information. Finally, the Exchange holds a collection of sample documents, for example the various forms of legal agreements which have been used to establish co-operatives.

Because innovatory developments are so widely diffused and localised, the staff have to spend a good deal of time extending the Exchange's own information networks among those working in housing and economic development. However, from the start the Exchange decided to be highly selective in its choice of projects on which information would be collected, to avoid being swamped with an unmanageable mass of information. So initially, the staff drew on their own experience and contacts to establish a list of about 100 new developments whose successes and difficulties would be relevant to other projects.

Then a model project was identified to illustrate each development. Over time this has expanded as new developments and further model projects emerge, so by the time of our research there were about 250 projects on the computer file. The staff of these projects are asked to supply basic information to the Exchange which also obtains any relevant documentation. This written material is then available for consultation by users. The project descriptions are updated annually so there is continuing contact between the projects and the Exchange.

The Information Exchange is used by a wide range of organisations, community housing developers, city and state development agencies, foundations and professionals working on local housing and economic development. The sorts of questions which it addresses include various sources of church and foundation support potentially available for particular developments; which community-based organisations have experience of managing housing directly; the latest situation with regard to federal funding for various forms of low-income housing and the various methods by which elderly persons' housing schemes might be financed.

The Information Exchange also publishes a bi-monthly newsletter, a monthly checklist on important new trends and practices and a series of technical bulletins (a recent example discussed how the funds available for the preservation of historic buildings might be used to create low-income housing). Its computer also has an electronic noticeboard on which user organisations can advertise jobs, request information from other projects and generally get in touch with people and organisations which may be useful to them.

Apart from its foundation funding, the Exchange obtains some income from user fees and has the long term aim of becoming self-supporting. However, Shabecoff told us, '...*on the whole the private sector was not interested in supporting us, except some financial institutions who wanted to fund something locally and needed to check out whether similar projects had worked elsewhere*'. So, as most of its users are not commercial organisations, it has to keep its fees at a fairly low level. At the time of our research. for example, the basic annual subscription was only $50 and computer time cost $40 per hour for community groups and $70 for others. Other fees were at a similarly modest level.

The Foundation for Housing Experiments

Organisations with a national scope of operation can have many functions beyond exchanging information. One fact that the innovative projects discussed in this book highlight is that there is no clear line between traditional and new forms of housing provision. The issues which locally-based housing groups are taking up cross the established limits of housing policies and include matters such as the combination of living and working space, collective forms of living and the flexible use of space. In this situation, practical experiments have an important role to play – trying out new ideas 'on the ground'.

It is in this context that the Stichting Experimenten Volkshuisvesting (Experimental Housing Foundation) must be viewed. It is a unique body which has been established in the Netherlands to help support and evaluate promising examples of housing innovation. Professor Helga Fassbinder, one of the consultants for our project and a member of the foundation's board, told us about its work. It began in 1982 and was established by the State Secretary at the Housing Ministry (the equivalent to the British Minister of Housing). The Minister at the time was a Social Democrat but the succeeding centre-right government decided that the foundation was a useful innovation and has continued to fund it. This illustrates the broad social support which there is in the Netherlands for housing experiments, also reflected in the composition of the commission which decides what projects the Foundation will support.

The commission has about 10 independent members who serve without salary for a two year term and are appointed by the Minister. The members represent a wide range of housing interests. At the time of our research in 1987 two came from the housing associations, two were academics, two were mayors, two came from the building industry and one each from the main tenants' federation and from a women's housing group. The Foundation's budget covers its running costs and its direct support to projects. It has a full time paid secretary plus (by 1989) eight staff. A lot of the secretary's time is spent publicising what the organisation does. In 1987 its annual budget was 3m guilders.

About two thirds of this is spent on running the organisation. Professor Fassbinder commented: *'This is a very bad split, many members of the commission aren't very pleased about it but the Ministry supports the secretary because the value of the organisation for the Ministry is public relations'*. Apart from its support to groups, the Foundation also commissions small-scale research reports which survey specific areas of housing activity. These help the commission to identify new developments which it may then wish to aid.

The Foundation does not provide core funding for projects. It will only support projects which are able to obtain the major finance that they require from other sources, itself contributing supplementary grants to meet costs which cannot be funded in any other way because of the experimental nature of the projects. Normally, a fixed grant is provided for each project, usually from 30,000 to 90,000 guilders. In some cases, the Foundation funds external advisers when these are necessary for a project to be implemented.

Each funded project is also evaluated by outside researchers who examine the potential to apply it elsewhere. About 15 to 20,000 guilders per project is spent on this. The conclusions which the Foundation draws from these reports are presented to the Ministry of Housing. The hope is that this will then feed into policy formation. The Foundation also gives some projects support by arranging for them to be exempted from regulations which inhibit their experimental nature. Several of the projects discussed in this book have been supported by the Foundation, for example, the Half World scheme, the Woonwinkel and Buurtbeheer Oliemolens.

Over 50 projects have been supported by the Foundation. Much attention has been paid to analysing how dwellings are built, lived in and managed. Particular support has been given to projects which aim to develop forms of co-operation between the participants in the process of housing provision. New forms of tenure and housing management and housing for special groups, such as the elderly, are also regarded as important. The objective of increasing tenant influence over housing is seen as an important criterion for the Foundation's backing.

Initially, the Foundation had to obtain Ministry approval to fund specific projects but it now has greater independence. Nevertheless, Professor Fassbinder told us that one of the earlier priorities, private sector improvement, had *'come from the Ministry, it is very concerned now about this unsolved problem. But we would not have chosen it, it's a rather dull subject. We have also resisted work on technological innovation but it has been pushed by the director of the Ministry research department who is an observer at our meetings. However, the issue of women's emancipation is disliked by the Ministry but it has been pushed through by the women on the commission. In short, we bargain with the Ministry about the programme'.*

Most funding still comes from the Ministry but the private sector is now being approached and it is expected to make major contributions in future. Five programmes have now been developed; within each of them, projects are grouped under a number of themes. In brief, the programmes are:-

▶ *Management of post-war housing estates*; themes include the development and use of information systems in housing and estate management; market oriented rent policies (which include experiments to introduce larger rent differentials into social housing by rent pooling); market oriented housing improvement policies; and projects relating to upgrading the quality of post-war estates.

▶ *Housing for the elderly* ; themes include improved understanding of the needs of the elderly and making advanced provision for eventual old age in new building design; combining housing and services for the elderly, allowing them to live independently; and owner-occupation as a tenure for the older citizen (this latter theme mainly concerns new financing schemes).

▶ *Promoting individual home ownership*; this programme was initially concerned with private housing improvement. Its change of emphasis reflects current government housing policy interests. Themes include experimental forms of ownership of new housing; the sale of rental housing; and financing private housing improvement.

▶ *Women's emancipation*; this programme aims to increase women's influence over all aspects of housing provision. Projects relate to the training of female caretakers and of repair and maintenance workers; combining working and living quarters; and employing women housing association managers. A second major theme concerns the design of housing and the layout of housing estates to reflect women's needs.

▶ *Miscellaneous projects*; these include a 'housing park' for the elderly (combining housing with recreation and education provision); and a project to increase the housing in inner city shopping streets while improving safety.

By 1989 the Foundation's priorities, listed above, showed a marked shift away from some of its earlier concerns such as 'open building' and projects concerned with housing design and quality. At the same time, the range of projects which it is funding has become more restricted. In general, the history of the Foundation suggests that a more systematic approach to experiments in housing provision would also be valuable in Britain in the current era of major housing policy changes.

Both Britain and the Netherlands are moving towards a more market oriented housing system which, it is claimed, will be more flexible and adaptable to changing needs. But housing for lower-income groups – who have similarly changing needs but have limited resources to spend on housing – must not be ignored. The Foundation's recent changes in emphasis suggest that in the Netherlands, as in Britain, there is a danger that such lower-income housing needs will be increasingly marginalised and/or translated into a series of 'special need' categories such as 'the elderly', 'immigrants/guest workers/ethnic minorities', and 'women'.

National Organisation of Housing Groups

The Landelijke Organisatie Belangengroepen Huisvesting (the Dutch name) is a housing organisation whose closest British parallel is Shelter. Harry Windmuller, a worker with the project told us, *'we work for people who are searching for shelter'*. It was founded in the mid-seventies, arising out of several projects concerning housing for small (one and two person) households, and had a general remit to assist low and moderate-income households and others who were disadvantaged in the housing market. It combined a lobbying role with a great deal of practical work supporting specific housing schemes.

At the time it was founded there was a severe general shortage of housing and the Organisation focused on pressing for more social housing to be built. Later, it also became concerned with issues of housing quality, costs and affordability, tenant allocation and tenants' rights. It has continued to focus on special needs groups, in particular, the young and the elderly. But the Organisation is also concerned with national housing campaigns which it plans with similar bodies and tenant interest groups. These campaigns have concerned – among others – rent policies, the level of annual rent increases, security of tenure and the problem of high heating costs.

The Organisation has a central office in Amsterdam and five regional offices. The headquarters carries out most lobbying and the other offices work on specific projects, offering aid and advice to individuals and groups and feeding information for use in lobbying to the centre. Interestingly, although it has a little self-generated income from members' contributions, subsidies from local authorities and from the services it provides, over 60 per cent of its funding comes from the Ministry of Housing. Despite this there has been no political interference in the Organisation's work; it has established good contacts with all the major political parties and this, plus the multi-party

Dutch political system, helps to ensure its independence.

It is a small organisation, with three policy workers at the centre, where 10 staff work in all, and one consultant at each of the regional offices, assisted by at least one (and usually three) voluntary workers. This enables it to operate with a minimum of bureaucracy and hierarchy. When specialist work is required it will often employ consultants to assist it (as we saw in the case of the housing conversion programme discussed in the last chapter).

Proposals about new themes for courses, campaigns or other activities often come from the regional workers and are then discussed by all staff. Each of the three centre policy staff has overall responsibility for one of the Organisation's major areas of activity: education and publicity; policy and lobbying; and regional co-ordination. It is a membership organisation – members pay an income-related fee from 10 guilders a year upwards. Apart from individual members, groups which are working in the interests of tenants and the homeless can join. Organisations such as housing associations are not eligible for membership but can become financial supporters.

At the time of our research, the Organisation was involved in a number of schemes. One major campaign concerned research into the extent of the housing shortage in the Netherlands. For several years information had been collected and publicised concerning the number of people on housing waiting lists. In 1987 this was estimated at 1.6 million, of whom 60 per cent belonged to lower-income households (with a gross monthly income of less than 2,000 guilders). Other campaigns were aimed at expanding social house building and halting the trend to lower space standards in new housing as well as opposing cuts in housing allowance expenditure.

Another key issue concerned the market in rented rooms, particularly important for young people. Studies were published about how such rooms were let, how rents were and should be calculated and about tenants' rights. Housing for the elderly had also become a central campaigning issue. The Organisation aimed to co-operate here with elderly persons' groups; projects were mainly concerned with developing group housing schemes.

The Organisation was also active in assisting other forms of group housing, usually in relation to the type of building conversion, self-help and tenant management schemes which we discussed in the last chapter. Similar themes formed the core activities of its regional consultants (plus others such as campaigns concerning houseboats and women's issues in housing). There was a direct link between lobbying for policy changes and the Organisation's involvement in providing practical help to a range of housing groups.

Some time after our research was completed in 1987 the Organisation and two other national housing groups decided to merge. As a first step they formed a federal organisation. The activities of the three constituent organisations are complementary. The other two are the National Tenants' Organisation (NVH) and LOS which is mainly concerned with assisting tenant groups in urban renewal and housing improvement schemes. The three groups are already working together on national housing campaigns. It is expected that the new federation will establish a much stronger, democratically-organised body of tenants and homeless people. In addition, with the more efficient use of finances and personnel, a better service will be provided for local tenant organisations and for other initiatives taken by housing consumers. The name of the new body will be De Nederlandse Woonbond and it is to be set up with 100,000 members in 1990.

It is envisaged that the core funding for the new organisation will come from central government. The aim is, however, to become more independent. The merger was encouraged by the Secretary of State for Housing as he wanted to create structures for negotiating housing issues at national and local levels. Here, negotiations between all the parties concerned could take place over important housing issues such as the annual, governmentally determined rent rises. The federation however wants the independent role of housing consumers to be recognised in the relevant housing legislation.

The Wohnbund Organisation

The Wohnbund was founded in 1983 by a group of West German housing academics and professionals who were already involved in a range of housing initiatives (the organisation is sub-titled 'association for the support of housing policy initiatives'). In 1983 housing problems were rapidly worsening, partly because of changes in policy, such as the privatisation of social housing, but also due to market developments, such as tenure conversion in the private sector. At the same time, grassroots housing initiatives were increasing, often with professional support.

The aim of the Wohnbund, as expressed in its initial position papers, is to counter the main current in housing markets and policies, to end the isolation of local tenants' groups from each other and to exchange and extend information and experience across the whole country. It also attempts to bring together professionals, academics and politicians in a single network whose function is to transmit ideas and provide professional assistance. Wohnbund's overall objective is to increase the stock of affordable housing and to develop user control over housing. So it provides the means of improving contacts between different areas across the country and articulates alternative housing policies.

Professor Klaus Novy, a consultant for our project and one of the leading lights in the organisation, told us, ' *"Wohnbund" can be translated as "housing" or "home" union which, in the German tradition of social movements, has*

135

two meanings. The first refers to a linking or binding together of housing professionals, the second to the ties between the home and its users'. By 1989 its membership was over 300, mostly individuals plus a few groups. In the main it is an organisation of individual professionals, planners and architects plus a few economists and lawyers.

Wohnbund was initially organised into a number of working groups which each dealt with a particular theme. These partly reflected local initiatives and partly issues of national importance. The groups covered tenure conversion, co-operatives and the social ownership of housing, models for alternative forms of housing finance (out of which emerged the Foundation for Neighbourhood Development in Hessen), pre-war workers' estates (out of which the Rheinpreussensiedlung emerged), self-help, and women and housing (these last two groups were less successful due to the wide scope of their concerns).

All these groups worked at a national level but it soon became impractical to meet regularly due to the size of the country. Most groups eventually developed a strong regional or state bias in their active membership. So activities were then decentralised. The organisation has a central office in Frankfurt which co-ordinates activities and publishes a Wohnbund Journal, the main medium for exchanging information nationally. It also organises international conferences (four so far) at which a wide range of projects and ideas are presented. The financing of this office is quite shaky and most work is done on a voluntary basis. Conferences are mainly self-financing and have also received some grant aid.

Wohnbund also has regional organisations which are directly concerned with providing advice and assistance to local initiatives. These regional boards mainly consist of professionals, most of whom already have their own practices as progressive architects or planners. Using the Wohnbund title these professionals bid for contracts or grants from state and local governments on behalf of the tenants in projects which they wish to support or to carry out research (for example, on tenant participation or on new forms of social ownership). Some are paid via a special social security scheme for unemployed academics.

So far, a fully functional regional office is only operative in North-Rhine Westphalia, which has a strong social democratic tradition – and thus readily available funding – and perhaps more housing activists than other areas. There is also an office in Hessen, but not apparently very active, and one is being established in West Berlin. Due to the differences in the political and socio-economic structures of the Lander it is not surprising that the regional support networks are having to be developed in different ways.

Wohnbund emphasises that it is independent of all political parties. It mainly acts as a lobby group responding to issues which it directly encounters in its advice and assistance work. As the main focus is on the regional networks, national campaigns are limited. The few that have been launched are concerned with 'progressive' housing solutions such as social ownership; alternative sources of finance; and changes in legislation which will reduce the stock of low cost accommodation.

Discussion

In the first chapter of this book we argued that the current growth of a mass of mainly small-scale and localised housing innovations is no mere coincidence. Despite their immense diversity they can all be seen as responses to a situation in which the ability of 'mainstream' housing policies and institutions to deliver decent and affordable housing to low and moderate-income housing consumers has come under increasing pressure. Many of these innovations may fail, some may succeed but remain only of minor and local importance.

However, others are likely to grow in importance and be recognised as useful additions to established sources of housing provision. In order for this to occur, projects have to obtain financial, technical and other resources. As we have seen in many of the cases described in this book, the role of support organisations and the expertise of their staff is often central to the success or failure of a project. However, the types of organisation which we have discussed in this chapter also have a vital role to play in promoting housing innovations more widely.

The national organisations described in this chapter illustrate some of the different forms that this support can take, from purely information exchange to providing financial support and expertise and organising national campaigns on behalf of lower-income households. Often co-operation occurs with other organisations involved in providing housing and, of course, governments also have an important role to play.

However, not all innovations solely concern lower-income housing. The Dutch Experimental Housing Foundation, for example, is clearly trying to combine private interests, such as those of building companies and housing associations, with the interests of government and tenants. A central theme is the general recognition that housing markets and policies are changing rapidly and that the established structures of housing provision are in a state of flux.

A new 'balance' is being sought, with fewer subsidies and state involvement and greater reliance on the private or semi-private sectors. This helps to explain the interest of house builders, financial institutions and social housing landlords in experiments with new forms of housing provision. Increased consumer involvement is now deemed necessary in order to discover what future market demands will be. One consequence is that organisations which work on behalf of lower-income housing consumers may find themselves being taken more seriously. They may be consulted on new policies or legislation, be included in various official bodies, receive financial support and so on. In short, they may begin to be incorporated into the housing policy 'establishment' – as appears to be happening to the three housing pressure groups in the Netherlands. However, while these forms of recognition may increase, they are not necessarily accompanied by an extension or even the maintenance of mainstream housing policies which aid lower-income households. In the Netherlands, with falling rates of social house building and sharply rising rents, this is certainly the case.

Interestingly, much of the funding for these organisations comes from government. This certainly applies to the Experimental Housing Foundation and the National Organisation of Housing Groups in the Netherlands, although not to the Community Information Exchange. However, both the Dutch organisations are expected to obtain a larger share of their funding from other sources in future. State funding is also sought by the Wohnbund in the form of research grants and development contracts on behalf of low-income housing consumers.

This also occurs in the Netherlands where progressive architects and planners are providing technical assistance and in the USA where fundraising skills are also particularly well developed. But, with the privatisation of housing policies and agencies, will the increasing pressure on support organisations to be self-financing conflict with their continued ability to serve low-income populations who cannot afford to pay the full cost of such services?

To summarise, there are several distinct functions of these organisations, although many combine two or more of them in their operations. These are:-

▶ Systematic collection and dissemination of information about innovative projects and examples of 'best practice'.

▶ The establishment of support networks, linking projects which have similar objectives, methods of working and problems to resolve.

▶ Drawing on the experience of the projects to lobby government and the private sector for the necessary resources for housing innovation and for the removal or modification of inappropriate and unnecessary regulations, practices and procedures.

▶ Providing supplementary assistance to enable experimental housing projects to be developed and the systematic evaluation of their problems, achievements and wider applicability.

▶ Acting as a focal point for new thinking about housing needs and the means of housing provision; attempting to look beyond the often narrow and unduly limited confines of current policy debates to explore more radical solutions.

▶ Perhaps the most difficult objective; acting as a link between localised housing groups (including those which are not involved in innovatory schemes) to build campaigns for progressive changes in housing legislation and policies.

None of the organisations discussed in this chapter employed a large staff and none of them had enormous budgets. But they were all making important contributions to one or more of the above objectives in their respective countries. Britain has, of course, several organisations which act as lobby groups, provide assistance and so on. But rather few of them have a particular concern with promoting and assisting housing *innovations*. Many concentrate, understandably, on working within the established system of housing provision and its policy framework. Yet if, as we have argued, this system is increasingly unable or unwilling to meet the needs of the less privileged housing consumer, there is a strong case for some greater diversion of attention and resources to the promotion and evaluation of new developments which are marginal in terms of their current significance but which may act as the prototypes for the future.

8. Towards New Forms of Housing Provision?

I n this final chapter we first want to return to the broad themes relating to the contemporary restructuring of housing provision and the significance of innovations in this context which we discussed in chapter one. We shall then outline some of the most important common features which are shared by many of the projects which we have described and the lessons which can be learnt from their achievements and their limitations. Finally, we will suggest a way in which innovatory forms of low- and moderate-income housing provision could be further encouraged, supported and developed in Britain, drawing on the experience of some of the projects which have been analysed in this book.

An alternative future for social housing?

In chapter one we suggested that, for a variety of economic, social and political reasons, the relatively settled system of post-war housing provision has increasingly come under stress. Problems of housing affordability, access and quality have re-emerged on a large scale, particularly in respect to low- and moderate-income households. We argued that, when viewed as a whole, the mass of usually small-scale and locally-based housing innovations now apparent in Britain and in many other countries could be seen as a response to the failure of the conventional system of housing to provide for lower-income housing needs. We pointed out that since 1980 the British government had embarked on a radical reconstruction of lower-income housing provision, the latest stage of which is now incorporated in the 1988 Housing Act and in subsequent legislation reforming local authority housing finance.

With few exceptions, the critical response to these developments has been mainly of a defensive nature. This is partially the product of the blinkered vision which characterises much contemporary housing debate.

However, there is now an urgent need to go beyond a purely piecemeal and reactive response, to formulate an alternative vision and a new agenda for British housing.

Such an agenda would have to consider the whole range of housing provision – how it is financed, constructed, allocated, paid for and lived in. However, our concern in this book has been with a more limited range of issues centring on low- and moderate-income housing. One obvious justification for this limited focus is simply that current trends in housing markets and policies have a notable – and increasingly uneven – impact, sustaining and even increasing the quality of housing enjoyed by the better off while creating a growing housing crisis for those in low wage employment or dependent on social security benefits.

If a new agenda for housing is to make any real impact, it must also be grounded in the everyday experiences and realities of those whom it aims to assist. This means that it must grow out of the struggles, successes and failures of those who are now attempting to develop new forms of lower-income housing provision, rather than ignoring or dismissing this experience.

As we have seen in this book most of these housing innovations have their limitations. Opinions may differ about whether, in an ideal world, developments such as tenant management or self-help housing would be preferable to a reformed but essentially traditional system of mass social housing provision. However, this is really a side issue in the current political and economic climate. To reject, because of their obvious limitations, the potential significance of the innovations we have described would simply, in practice, leave the way clear for an intensification of the direction taken by national housing policies in the last decade – and for all their negative consequences.

Of course, a new agenda for lower-income housing must consist of more than a collection of disconnected, fragmentary bright ideas. It must try to outline the basic aims, objectives and methods which would characterise housing policies and practices. Some of these themes are already emerging as common features of many of the schemes which we have examined in this book. We shall now list these briefly, referring back to some of the projects which best illustrate their significance.

▶ *Affordability*: This is perhaps the most obvious characteristic of the projects which we have examined but it is worth underlining because it is the fundamental objective of most of the projects and the main reason for many of the specific innovations which have occurred. The objective of realising affordable housing for lower-income households is central to a broad range of initiatives concerned, for example, to lower building costs and modify standards, to adopt innovative financing schemes and to use self-help.

▶ **Securing low cost housing**: This objective follows from the previous characteristic. In Britain, the USA and West Germany and even now in the Netherlands, the supply of low cost housing is diminishing. Reasons for this include reduced subsidies for such housing as well as the conversion of private rental housing for upper-income use and the privatisation of existing social housing. Projects such as the Foundation for Neighbourhood Development in West Germany, social home ownership in the Netherlands and the mutual housing associations in the USA illustrate some of the new attempts to create a stock of good quality, affordable and permanently available lower-income housing.

An important issue is self-sufficiency in the face of the privatisation of social housing now occurring. New ways are being sought to realise a form of social housing which has some degree of independence from market developments and state policies.

▶ **Alternative sources of housing investment**: Given the declining levels of public investment in lower-income housing and the lack of any sign that this trend is likely to be reversed in the near future, the need to obtain other sources of finance becomes crucial if the supply of lower-income housing is to be increased on any significant scale. There is, of course, much debate in Britain about the potential role of private finance in this context but still relatively little practical experience of its scope and limitations. In the USA, as projects such as the Local Initiatives Support Corporation, the Enterprise Loan Fund, the Chicago Housing Partnership and the South Shore Bank illustrate, some clear lessons are beginning to emerge.

▶ **Self-help**: Self-help is a feature of many of the projects which we have described. It is mainly used as a cost saving exercise. Self-help can concern the design and development process, building and improvement works or management and maintenance. Self-help can become quite institutionalised: in West Germany project developers normally have to contribute 15 per cent of total development costs to be eligible for other funding. In projects, such as the Linden co-operative in Hannover, self-build is being used to replace this down payment for low-income users. In a different way, *open bouwen* institutionalises self-help by allowing future occupiers to work – to varying degrees – at finishing their building.

▶ **Developments from 'below'**: As we have noted at several points in the book, many of the projects were based on initiatives taken by grassroots or at least locally-based organisations and groups. In part, this was simply a response to the failure of 'top down' policies and programmes. But it was also the product of dissatisfaction with many aspects of such 'mass' housing programmes; with the type of housing they have provided; how it has been managed and its costs. Sharply contrasting examples of such neighbourhood-based development are provided – in one city – by the Nehemiah Project and by the Urban Homesteading Assistance Board aided tenant co-operatives. Other examples include self-help rehabilitation projects in Berlin and the Rheinpreussensiedlung.

▶ *Links to neighbourhood revitalisation*: Several further features of many of the projects are closely related to their local origins. One of these concerns the role of housing development in helping to reverse urban decay and decline. This objective was especially evident in many of the US projects, probably because such decline is more extensive and extreme here than in the other two countries. Good examples include the programmes supported by the South Shore Bank and the Nehemiah Project. Most European projects which have strong area-based aspects, such as the Foundation for Neighbourhood Development, social home ownership in Rotterdam and self-help rehabilitation projects in Berlin are more concerned to combat gentrification.

▶ *Responses to new types of housing needs*: Another characteristic of several of the projects which was linked to their 'bottom up' rather then 'top down' origins was that they were responses to needs, some of them brought about by changing economic and social circumstances, which conventional forms of mass housing provision largely ignore. There are, in particular, two divisions which most conventional housing enshrines and even reinforces; that between the workplace and the home and that between the household and the community.

Although most people accept and may even welcome such divisions, there is a growing range of households which do not. Projects like Woonkollectief Purmerend and several other schemes supported by the Dutch Experimental Housing Foundation involve such groups, including those which focus on the elderly and women.

▶ *Consumer control*: A further feature of conventional housing provision, whether in the private or the social sector, is the lack of control by its consumers over its design, construction and, in the case of rental housing, its management. Many of the projects which we have described were attempting in some way or another to alter this situation, to break down and restructure, for example, landlord/tenant or developer/client relationships. Projects such as *open bouwen*, tenant management in Jersey City and Amsterdam, the Interim Tenant Lease and Nehemiah schemes and the self-build projects in all three countries illustrate this tendency. Note, too, the interest of private sector institutions in such developments for the reasons already discussed. The Dutch Experimental Foundation's recent programme illustrates this point.

▶ **Enabling organisations**: All forms of housing provision require what might be described as an organisational and resource infrastructure. Financial resources have to be secured; organisations established; skills acquired; and political support sought. Once these mechanisms are established they tend to be relatively impervious to radical change, certainly to change 'from below' and to innovations which may not be in the interests of those who control and benefit from their current forms.

Many of the types of innovatory projects which we have discussed in this study do not fit easily – if at all – into the conventional housing infrastructure. This is why there is such a crucial need to develop new organisations to support and sustain housing innovation by providing practical skills and access to resources; establishing information networks; lobbying for political support and – if necessary – institutional and legislative change. The experience of organisations such as the Local Initiatives Support Corporation, the Dutch Experimental Housing Foundation and housing pressure groups, the Wohnbund, and the Community Information Exchange illustrate the range of needs and the response they are receiving.

In many ways, the features of the housing innovations which we have listed above are closely interrelated. At the same time, not all projects display all these characteristics. So it is perhaps a mistake to attempt any further generalisations about them. However, we do believe that many of the projects which we have discussed seem to point to the possible emergence of a new or alternative system of social housing. For some this new system involves a greater emphasis on the market, for others a reorganisation of state provision. Yet others may look to a system which lies 'between the state and the market'.

Our view is different. For, rather than being oriented to the state or the market, or even lying between the state and the market, what is significant about many of the projects is their attempt to provide, in however limited and partial a way, forms of housing which break with some of the rules, constraints and adverse consequences of state *and* market dominated mass housing provision.

Essentially, these innovations are attempting to shift the locus of control over housing away from state bureaucracy and from the institutions of the market towards its consumers. This means that they are trying to produce housing which serves the interests of consumers rather than those of politicians, state managers or the various sectors of the housing industry.

These interlinked objectives influence every aspect of housing provision, affecting design, construction, financing, management and – most crucially – the final price to the consumer.

What can be learnt from innovations?

While innovation at the margin may be tolerated – and even encouraged – by both the state and the market, there is no guarantee that an alternative system of lower-income housing provision will emerge on a major scale. As we have seen, most projects have had to fight hard to succeed even in a small way. Many may remain of no more than marginal significance. Moreover, insofar as the types of innovation, which we have described, seriously challenge the existing institutions and interests which control housing provision, they are likely to meet some stiff opposition.

But only some of the difficulties encountered stemmed from outright opposition by existing institutions and interests. Others were the consequence of continued dependency on such institutions and interests and the limited ability and/or wish of unorganised housing consumers to change their role in the housing system.

While the established housing system imposes considerable restraints, there are some positive lessons to be learnt from this study of housing innovations:-

▶ *Initiatives from the users*: The constraints of a top down approach have been mentioned several times. Most of the projects discussed in this book were initiated by users. Increasing user control over housing provision is imperative in order to respond to rapidly changing patterns of need. Old concepts of family living are breaking down and the outcome of current social, economic and demographic changes is very uncertain. More attention must therefore be paid to user demands and less taken for granted.

However, we are not arguing that all initiatives can, or should, come solely from the users. In practice, it tends to be the better educated (not necessarily in terms of formal qualifications) and the more physically able who get involved in experimental projects and other housing activism. Many others have their needs ignored or may not even be able to express them clearly or see what the alternatives to existing forms of provision might be.

A final point in this context is to emphasise again the key role of enabling organisations. Making consumer control a central element in housing innovation does not mean that consumers should simply be left to 'get on with it', without the necessary support.

▶ *Promotion of social housing*: To allow housing choice for all, a stock of low cost accommodation is essential. This requires state subsidies as well as some form of collective ownership. Only with such ownership can the stock be preserved for future generations of low-income households. Also, social housing has often provided a sector within which innovatory developments occur that are later taken up by the private market (for example, warden assisted elderly persons dwellings).

Almost all the projects which attempted to ensure that their housing remained permanently available for lower-income households faced great – and sometimes insurmountable – difficulties. In some cases, for example the Mount Vernon projects, such attempts seemed half-hearted at best. In other cases, such as the Nehemiah Project and some of the European self-build schemes, lower-income residents understandably failed to see why they should be excluded from the gains resulting from house price inflation which more privileged groups enjoyed.

In this context, the experience of the Rotterdam social home ownership scheme is interesting. It did have rigidly enforced and effective rules which maintained the availability of the housing for lower-income households. However, the incentive for people to join the scheme, namely below market sales prices, disappeared when house prices fell with the collapse of the housing market. This lesson can also be applied to individual schemes of lower-income home ownership. Such households not only gain from house price inflation, they may also lose if prices fall. Those on low-incomes are normally the first who are forced to default on mortgage payments or sell up when conditions worsen and, in circumstances of market collapse, they may end up with considerable debt burdens.

▶ *Democratic management and accountability*: As some of the projects in this book illustrate, self-help usually places heavy burdens on households which may already be highly stressed. The examples of the Half World scheme and Jersey City tenant management show just how important resident commitment is. Given these factors, rather than concentrate solely on promoting self-help in housing management or direct and unpaid tenant participation, we suggest that a more general objective should be to introduce more democratic management structures which increase resident control over professional management. Insofar as residents do themselves become the managers, they should be trained and paid to perform this role and be accountable to the tenants as a whole, as happened in the Jersey city scheme.

▶ *Flexible needs versus quality and standards*: Several of the innova-

147

tive projects, especially those which required some government assistance, were hampered by official policies and regulations designed for conventional housing, which were ill-adapted to their needs. For example, such problems were experienced by the Dutch building conversion projects and several other self-build schemes. Tenant management in Jersey City was similarly hedged around with federal regulations which greatly limited its budgetary discretion and the full cost-reducing potential of *open bouwen* could not be realised due to rigid government rules relating to housing quality and other matters. Similar problems dogged the co-operative programme in New York. Conversely, the experience of the Nehemiah Project and the Chicago Partnership illustrates how successful some schemes have been in finding ways round this problem.

However, setting housing quality standards raises difficult issues. Current arguments against strict official regulation of housing quality coincide with a more general trend to reduce some standards. This leads on to the issue of who is to define and set such standards – government, the users or the private sector? In any case, standards are much influenced by the ability and willingness to pay for them. To take just one example, one aim of *open bouwen* is to allow users to choose the level of quality which they require. Some critics of this scheme are worried that it will lead to the official standard being set at a minimal level (and subsidies provided accordingly) and that 'choice' will, in fact, be determined solely by residents' ability to pay.

Somewhere a path has to be found between the need to have flexible regulations, better adapted to emerging patterns of housing needs and the requirement to achieve a good basic standard of housing provision.

Reforming subsidies: The limits of private finance were noted in chapter four. Apart from some charitable funding, private institutions will only invest where there is a high probability of making a commercial return. This means that they can never substitute entirely for the public sector if the resulting housing is to be affordable by low- and moderate-income households.

The constraints imposed by private funding have some further consequences, too. Low cost rehabilitation – not new building – tends to be the rule. Areas of higher priced housing and those which are severely deteriorated have to be avoided. Development costs need to be reduced, for instance, by obtaining professional and building services cheaply. Reduced subsidies tend to result in projects having to choose between providing lower quality housing concentrated in limited and socially segregated localities or providing housing which is not affordable by many lower-income households.

Continued dependence – to some degree – on subsidies was a feature of virtually all the projects which we visited. This dependence limited the projects in two ways. First, as the amount of subsidy available has been declining, the size of projects was restricted. Second, the dependency on state support through direct subsidies limited the extent to which projects could control their own development. Some projects have tried to circumvent these difficulties. In the case of the first limitation they have tried, as we have already noted, to tap other sources of assistance. In the case of the second limitation, they have tried to obtain forms of government assistance which do not come with so many 'strings' attached: many US projects used private sector, but tax-subsidised, finance for example.

Also, an increasing number of projects (such as the Hessen Foundation for Neighbourhood Development and the US mutual housing associations) have argued for the use of lump sum capital grants rather than annual subsidies which normally carry a mass of continuing regulations. Of course, the experience of the UK housing associations suggests that a regime of capital grants does not necessarily guarantee freedom from regulation!

One important objective for any reform of housing subsidies would be to place more emphasis on using them to encourage new building and to discourage the process of gentrification which adversely affects the supply of lower cost housing. In general, subsidy systems should encourage long-term investment rather than shorter-term speculative gains. This requires a change in the recent trend away from supporting new investment and towards subsidising consumption and the market exchange of the existing stock.

▶ *Extending the capacities of housing consumers*: Even if they are committed to exercising more control over their housing, consumers often lack the expertise, power and other resources which are required. Consumers may, for example, lack the professional skills needed to manage their housing and the economic and political power to gain the assistance which they require. In this context, the existence of organisations such as the Local Initiatives Support Corporation, the Neighborhood Reinvestment Corporation and the Dutch Experimental Housing Foundation have become crucial and the development of further such organisations needs to be encouraged. Housing users need to have access to expert advice and to practical education as well as to the sort of decentralised information network which the Community Information Exchange is providing. Finally, consumers need to develop a stronger political voice – the kind of lobbying which organisations like the Wohnbund and the Dutch housing pressure groups are engaged in.

Taken together, this is a formidable list of problems as well as possibilities. Many of the projects have had to modify, reduce or even abandon some of their initial objectives in the face of major difficulties. However, we want to stress our conclusion that this is not a valid reason to ignore what they have achieved or to dismiss their potential contribution to informing and assisting parallel developments in Britain and to stimulating new ideas and action. In the last part of this chapter we make a modest proposal of our own which might contribute to expanding the supply of lower-income housing in Britain.

Neighbourhood-based housing experiments in Britain

Our proposal combines several of the key features of the innovative projects which we have described in this book. But, equally importantly, we believe that it is consistent with some of the more positive and encouraging new ideas and projects which have already emerged in Britain. Despite our general concern about the narrow perspectives which dominate much of the British housing scene, we know that, especially at grassroots and local levels, there are innovative and creative responses. We wish to strengthen and add to these responses.

As we have noted, contemporary developments in housing policies and markets are reducing the supply of affordable housing for significant sections of the population. Moreover, despite the rhetoric which accompanies the break-up of council housing, there is no solid basis for believing that tenant choice or control will be enhanced by a mere change of landlord. In fact, it gives us reasons for fearing that security and affordability will be reduced. Our proposal is intended to counter such trends.

In outline, we suggest that an attempt is made to develop a *neighbourhood housing movement*, a network of existing and new locally-based organisations working together to expand the supply of housing for low- and moderate-income households. There are several reasons for the neighbourhood-based orientation. For example, as we have discovered, the nature of innovative housing projects is greatly influenced by specific local possibilities and constraints: the nature of the local housing markets, local politics, community-based activism and economic conditions. Only locally-based organisations can fully take account of such varied local conditions. At the same time, there is also a national framework of policies and legislation and a need to share and disseminate local experiences more widely. Hence, the need for a *national* network to link and sustain *local* initiatives.

The housing which would be developed by such a movement should, as far as possible, be permanently available for lower-income households. It should be affordable and designed, built and managed in ways which suit the needs of its occupants and which maximise their control over it. Of course, as we have seen repeatedly throughout this book, none of this will be easily achieved. So success will be a relative matter and will be seen as a cumulation of many small-scale achievements rather than a radical and large-scale reversal of current trends. The emphasis which we place on the need for a housing *movement* underlines this point.

Such a neighbourhood housing movement would seek to develop a wide range of housing, taking into account the growing need to combine home and work and new forms of group and communal living, as well as more 'conventional' life styles. This housing would be in differing forms of ownership. It may be rented from housing associations and local authorities, in co-operatives and forms of co-ownership or experimenting with wholly new tenures, such as 'socially controlled ownership'.

It would seek to link housing investment to a wider process of neighbourhood revitalisation and to exploit new sources of finance for lower-income housing. It would lobby and organise to obtain the financial and technical resources which it would require and to modify existing policies and procedures as necessary. It would seek to establish a growing number of locally-based housing developers and institutions committed to investing in areas where these developers are working. Finally, such a movement would act as a national focus to bring together the efforts and energies of the many, currently rather isolated, projects which are already attempting to find practical solutions to the low-income housing crisis.

The previous chapters of this book provide a mass of detail concerning some of the ways in which neighbourhood housing might be developed. For the reasons which we discussed in chapter one, we do not believe that it would be sensible to go further than we already have done in pointing out how this foreign experience might be of relevance in the British context. Any detailed blueprint for change is not likely to be worth more than the paper it is written on. However, we do think that some purposeful action will be necessary if we are to move '*beyond the fragments*' in housing, to develop a significant new agenda for lower-income housing *and* to begin to implement it.

In the current climate this means that we have to look to present housing organisations which already have a strong commitment to expanding lower-income housing supply, or which might be persuaded to take up this role, to initiate the sort of neighbourhood-based housing movement which we have outlined. The central element in such a movement would be the many, mostly small-scale, innovatory projects which already exist. But they are already heavily committed to their own work and often have little time or other resources to devote to anything else. However, there are some other organisations which could play leading roles in establishing the sort of alternative housing programme which we envisage. These include:-

▶ *Housing and housing related charities and pressure groups*: Many of them are already promoting or encouraging housing innovation. Some of these organisations might now consider whether there is more that they can do to co-ordinate and develop their efforts. They might also consider whether a part of the time and effort which they now put, necessarily but often rather fruitlessly, into defending existing forms of low-income housing when these are under attack, should be used to develop more positive projects.

▶ *Housing associations*: It is already clear that some housing associations (and not only the smaller ones) are deeply unhappy about the new roles which recent policy changes and new financial arrangements are pushing them towards. Many associations retain a strong commitment to the sort of consumer-oriented, locally-based housing developments which we have described in this book. If they are to achieve their objectives, and even perhaps survive in the long run, they need to build links with others committed to the same ends. They could contribute a great deal to the sort of neighbourhood housing movement which we have outlined.

▶ *Building societies*: Perhaps less obviously there are still some relatively small building societies which have not as yet been swallowed up by the giants of the industry and which, unlike these latter, retain strong links with their localities. They could potentially become a cornerstone of neighbourhood housing development, collecting local savings and using the new opportunities which are now open to them to attract other sources of investment that would be channelled into local housing and allied projects. In any event, this could well be in their long term interest for if such societies cannot carve out a specialised niche for themselves in the housing finance market they are not likely to survive.

▶ *Secondary housing co-operatives*: They could extend their role. Like the Wohnbund, or maybe the Community Information Exchange or the Experimental Housing Foundation, they could set up networks to support innovatory developments.

This is not an exhaustive or exclusive list. Many other housing related organisations could play valuable roles in helping to establish a neighbourhood housing development movement. However, there is one further very important set of organisations which could have a major contribution to make to a neighbourhood housing movement, namely the local authorities. To some extent the 1988 Housing Act might be seen, in theory at least, to encourage local councils to move away from direct housing provision to supporting other housing providers. These might include the sort of neighbourhood housing developers and managers which we envisage.

But we doubt whether many local authorities will feel inclined to initiate a neighbourhood housing movement or in practice be allowed by central government to take on such a role. Our impression is that change must now come from outside the public sector. Local authority involvement will be an additional, and indeed necessary, resource – but only if it comes without the sort of damaging restrictions which current national policies towards housing and local government increasingly impose.

Appendix I
Checklist of Projects

This is a list of all the major projects described in the book, together with brief details about them. They are listed in the order in which they are first discussed in detail in the text. The numbers in brackets refer to the pages where this discussion is to be found.

Tenant management in Jersey City
Very low-income tenants now managing the old, high density, public housing projects where they live. Began in the mid-seventies. (52–58)

The Half World housing project – Amsterdam
Tenant management in a new, low rise housing project. Began in the early 1980s. (58–63)

Local Initiatives Support Corporation
Established in 1980 by the Ford Foundation, this organisation provides technical support and finance for housing and other new investment in declining inner urban areas. It is based on the establishment of public/private partnerships and matches locally-raised funding with its own resources. (70–74)

The Enterprise Foundation
Founded in 1981 by a former real estate developer, it has broadly similar functions to those of the Local Initiatives Support Corporation. Aims to cross-subsidise its low-income housing work from commercial retail developments. (74–75)

The Chicago Housing Partnership
An interlinked series of initiatives and organisations which began in 1983, (including the **Chicago Equity Fund** and the **Community Equity Assistance Corporation**), involving a partnership between the public and private sectors and local communities, to build and rehabilitate low- and moderate-income housing in inner city neighbourhoods. Backed by the Local Initiatives Support Corporation. (75–79)

The South Shore Bank
A commercial bank, in a formerly declining area of Chicago, which combines commercial business with non- and limited-profit investment in lower-income housing and small businesses. Operating in its current form since the early 1970s. (79–82)

The Baltimore Housing Partnership
Established in 1984 by the mayor and local business to rehabilitate vacant housing for moderate-income owner-occupation. Minimises costs by innovative financing and obtaining building and professional services relatively cheaply. (82–85)

The Mount Vernon Apartment Improvement Program
A programme which, since 1979, has been rehabilitating large blocks of private rented apartments while retaining them for lower-income occupation. Supported by public and private finance and public subsidies, it involves the co-operation of tenants and landlords in deciding what improvements to carry out and how they should be paid for. (86–88)

The Nehemiah Plan
A large-scale programme, developed by East Brooklyn churches in the early 1980s and supported by New York state and city subsidies, to build single-family housing for purchase by people on a moderate-income. Located on derelict sites in one of the most devastated areas of New York City. (94–99)

Urban Homesteading Assistance Board and the Tenant Interim Lease Program
A programme, operative since 1978, in which the assistance board helps low-income tenants in landlord-abandoned properties to establish co-operative ownership. Aided by New York City council with some federal subsidies. (99–103)

Manna
A small-scale project based in Washington DC to rehabilitate derelict housing for moderate-income home ownership. Minimises costs by employing its own professional services and builders. Financially assisted by the city council and donations. Began in the early 1980s. (103–105)

Oliemolens Neighbourhood Management (Buurtbeheer Oliemolens)
Oliemolens is an experiment in the innovative use of government improvement subsidies, backed by the Dutch Experimental Housing Foundation (see chapter seven), to enable the area-based improvement of low-income owner-occupied housing. (105–106)

Open building
An approach to design and building, pioneered in the Netherlands, which separates 'shell' and 'infill'. Allows occupants greater freedom of design and potential cost-savings, through the use of self-help to complete the infill. (111–115)

Self-building in Rotterdam
Four projects in Rotterdam which involved – in varying degrees – people on a moderate-income building their own houses for owner-occupation. (115–116)

The Chorweiler estate – Cologne
A self-build project for new owner-occupied housing, aided by a local group of architects. (116–117)

Urban Homesteading Assistance Board – sweat equity projects
Began by assisting self-build rehabilitation of 12 blocks of apartment in New York City in the late 1970s, part of a federal demonstration programme. (117–118)

Self-help improvement in West Berlin
A city-supported programme, assisted by a non-profit welfare organisation, which

enables lower-income tenants to rehabilitate their buildings and convert them to co-operative ownership. One objective is to prevent possible gentrification or demolition of this housing. Operative since the early 1980s. (118–120)

The Linden Self-help Co-operative – Hannover

A co-operative, founded in 1982, to purchase and improve dwellings in an urban renewal area. Prospective residents carry out renovations themselves to minimise costs and retain property in low-income occupation. (120–121)

Self-building and housing conversions in the Netherlands

A feasibility project, begun in 1984, to examine ways of converting non-residential buildings for lower-income rental housing, using available social rented housing subsidies. Despite difficulties, some of the projects have since been realised. (121–123)

Woonwinkel – Tilburg

A co-operative project to rehabilitate housing for younger, low-income occupants. Began in 1983 with backing from the Experimental Housing Foundation (see chapter seven). (123-124)

Chapter 7. Organisations supporting housing innovation

Community Information Exchange

Established in 1983, with support from the National Urban Coalition, the exchange collects information on innovative housing projects and related material. Its comput-erised data base is accessible to subscribers; it also provides documentary material and publishes a newsletter. (127–130)

The Foundation for Housing Experiments (Stichting Experimenten Volkshuisvesting)

Established as an independent commission by the Dutch government in 1982, the foundation provides supplementary finance for experimental housing projects and evaluates them. Several of the Dutch projects discussed in this book have been aided in this way. (130–133)

National Organisation of Housing Groups (Landelijke Organisatie Belangengroepen Huisvesting)

Founded in the mid-seventies and supported by a government grant, this organisa-tion campaigns for low-income housing and provides aid and advice for tenants. Due to merge with two other housing pressure groups in 1990. (133–135)

Wohnbund ('Housing Union')

Founded in 1983 by German housing academics and professionals, the Wohnbund combines pressure group activity with professional assistance for tenants' and other activity. Organises conferences and publishes a journal. (135–137)

Appendix II
The Research Project

As explained in chapter one, the project on which this book is based was first suggested to us by the realisation that recent social, economic and political changes were resulting in some profound changes in housing markets and policies. In particular, conventional housing provision seemed decreasingly capable of delivering affordable and decent housing to lower-income households. In this context we were seeing, in many countries, a remarkable growth of mainly small-scale innovatory housing projects, all aiming, in one way or another, to respond to the growing mass of low- and moderate-income housing needs.

In the course of our previous cross-national housing research we had built up a long list of contacts in West Germany, the Netherlands and the USA – three countries where, it seemed, some of the most interesting developments were occurring. After informal discussions and correspondence with some of these contacts, we were able to identify six broad areas of housing innovation which the research would concentrate on. We were also able to persuade six housing experts, two in each country, to act as our consultants for the project.

The main stages of the research were as follows:-

1. We drew up a detailed brief for the consultants, asking them to prepare preliminary reports which set out the broad context of housing innovation in each of their countries, outlined the main areas of innovatory activity and provided brief details of specific projects and programmes which, in their view, best illustrated these developments.

2. These reports were discussed at a small seminar, held in London in March 1986. Participants included our consultants, members of our project Advisory Group and a range of British housing professionals from central and local government, the private and voluntary sectors and some housing academics. The main purpose of this meeting was to help us decide which of the many projects discussed in our consultants' reports were likely to be of greatest interest to British housing policy makers and practitioners.

3. Following this meeting we drew up a list of around 50 projects in the three countries which we wished to visit. With the aid of our consultants these projects were contacted and, in late 1986 and early 1987, we travelled to each country to carry out a series of in-depth interviews with project personnel and to clarify detailed aspects of their reports with the consultants.

4. Following transcription of the interviews, which ran into many hundreds of pages, we made a final selection of projects for detailed presentation in this book. In late 1987 and early 1988 the draft manuscript was circulated to the consultants for their comments and revisions.

159

Bibliography

In the course of the project we collected a great deal of documentary material. Because this book is intended, above all, to be of interest to those who have a practical concern with housing innovations (although, we hope, our academic colleagues will also find material of interest in it), we have not burdened the text with the normal scholarly apparatus of references and footnotes. But for those who are interested in these matters, we have listed some of the principal sources on which, together with our consultants' reports and our interviews, this book is based.

West Germany

Behrens, G. 'Die Stiftung Nachbarschaftliche Träger – Ein Wohnpolitisches Modell fur die 90er Jahren", Wohnbund, Darmstadt, 1986.

Brech, J. (ed) *Konzepte zur Wohnraumerhaltung, Beispiele-Modelle -Experimenten*, Bericht des 3. Internationaler Wohnbund Kongresses in Münster, 1986.

Bundes Forschungsanstalt für Landeskunde und Raumordnung *Nutzerbeteiligung im Wohnungsbau*, Heft 2 Informationen zur Raumentwicklung, Bonn, 1982.

Die Grünen, 'Stiftung zur Förderung Nachbarschaftliche Träger', Wiesbaden, 1984.

Frank, H., Schubert, D. *Lesebuch zur Wohnungsfrage*, Pahl Rugenstein Verlag, Cologne, 1983.

Hessischen Innenministerium, 'Hessen schaft neues wohnungsbaupolitisches Reformmodell', pressenmitteilung, June 1986.

IBA, *Step by Step: Careful Urban Renewal in Kreuzberg*, Internationale Bauausstellung, Berlin, 1987.

Kölner Planwerkstatt, *Wohnen in der Fremde –Zwei Projekte mit Türkische Familien in Köln*, Cologne, 1986.

Mietergenossenschaft Heimat in Gründung, *Vertrags- und Förderbedingungen*, Zwischenbericht, Nov. 1986.

Mühlich, E., 'Gewaltenteilung', *Bauwelt Heft 24*, 1986, 878-80.

Novy, K., *Genossenschafts-Bewegung: zur Geschichte und Zunkunft der Wohnreform*, Transit Buchverlag, Berlin, 1983.

Novy, K. et al. *Anders Leben, Geschichte und Zunkunft der Genossenschaftskultur*, Verlag JHW Dietz Nachf, Berlin/Bonn.

Segin, B. *Das Genossenschaftsprojekt Rheinpreussensiedlung*, Verlag für Wissenschaftliche Publikationen, Darmstadt, 1984.

Stattbau Informiert, Stattbau Stadtenwicklungs-GmbH, Berlin, 1984.

WerkStadt e.v. *Gemeinschaftliche Selbsthilfe und Stadterneuerung*, Verlag für Wissenschaftliche Publikationen, Darmstadt, 1985.

Wohnbund Journal, Heft 3, Sept 1984; Heft 4 Jan 1985; Heft 5 May 1985; Heft 10 1986.

The Netherlands

Berg, G J van., Mulder, LH., *Via Gebundeld Schilherstel op weg naar Gebundeld Beheer van de Eigen Woningen*, Voortgangsverslag Buurtbeheer Oliemolens Enschede, Rijksuniversiteit Groningen, 1985.

DHV, 'Onderzoek naar Knelpunten bij de Toepassing van het Principe Scheiding Drager-Inbouw in de Sociale Woningbouw, Samenvatting van drie deelstudies', 1983.

Fassbinder, H., "Experimentenbeleid: laten zien dat het ook ander kan', *Bouw 19*, 1985.

Klap, Ch., Metselaar, A., *Nieuwe Beheervormen in een nieuwe Fase*, (concept) OTB & SOMSO, 1986.

LOBH, *Zelfbeheer*, LOBH Verbouwreeks nr 5, Amsterdam, 1985.

LOBH, *Zelfwerkzaamheid*, LOBH Verbouwreeks nr 3, Amsterdam, 1986.

Lukez, P., *New Concepts in Housing Supports in the Netherlands*, Network USA, MIT, Cambridge, 1986.

Meulen, J van der, Habets, W., *Perspectieven voor Bewonersbelangenbehartiging binnen nieuwe Beheersvormen*, Technische Hogeschool Eindhoven-Bouwkunde, 1985.

SAR, *Huurderszelfwerkzaamheid: bewonersaktiviteiten enquete naar corporatiebeleid en* , Stichting Architecten Research, Eindhoven, 1985.

SAR, *Keyenburg: a Pilot Project*, Stichting Architecten Research, Eindhoven, 1985.

Schaijk, H van, Jansen, R,. *Buurtekonomie en Belangenstrijd van Uitkeringsge rechtigden*, BEEK, Purmerend, n.d.

Smeets, J. 'Experimenten in de Stadsvernieuwing: een Tour d'Horizon', *Bouw 19*, 1985.

Volkshuisvesting Rotterdam, *Maatschappelijk Gebonden Eigendom, Verleden, heden en toekomst*, Rotterdam, 1986.

USA

CLPHA, *Public Housing Today*, Council of Large Public Housing Authorities, Boston, 1986.

Housing Abandonment Task Force, *An End to Housing Abandonment: Saving Affordable Housing in Chicago Neighborhoods*, The Task Force, Chicago, 1984.

MANNA, *Housing For People Not Profit*, MANNA, Washington DC, 1986.

MPC, *Tenant Management: the Challenge and the Possibilities*, Metropolitan Planning Council, Task Force on the CHA, Chicago, 1986.

MUSCLE Inc., *Nonprofit Housing Developments that Work. Annual Report 1985-6*, MUSCLE INC, Washington DC, 1986.

Neighborhood Reinvestment Corporation, *A Progress Report to the United States Congress on the Mutual Housing Association National Demonstration*, 2nd edition, US Government Printing Office, Washington DC, 1985.

Neighborhood Reinvestment Corporation, *A Case Study from the Apartment Improvement Program: Mount Vernon, New York*, Neighborhood Reinvestment Corporation, Mount Vernon, n.d.

Pickman, J. et al., *Producing Lower Income Housing: Local Initiatives*, The Bureau of National Affairs Inc., Washington DC, 1986.

Rigby, R., *The Residents as Resource: a Public Housing Management Demonstration in Jersey City*, State of New Jersey, Trenton, 1982.

UHAB, *A Guide to Co-operative Ownership: The Homesteader's Handbook*, The Urban Homesteading Assistance Board, New York, 1984.

UHAB, *The Urban Homesteading Assistance Board 1974-1984. A Retrospective Report and Review*, The Urban Homesteading Assistance Board, New York, 1986.

UHAB, *Current Programs and Projects*, the Urban Homesteading Assistance Board, New York, 1987.

Swift, L., Pogge, J. *Neighborhood Reinvestment Partnership*, Woodstock Institute, Chicago, 1984.

Vidal, A., Howitt, A., Foster, K. , *Stimulating Community Development: an Assessment of the Local Initiatives Support Corporation*, Research Report R86-2, State, Local and Intergovernmental Center, Harvard University, Cambridge, 1986.

Woodstock Institute, *Evaluation of the Illinois Neighborhood Development Corporation*, US Government Printing Office, Washington DC, 1982.

Woodstock Institute, *Partners in Need: a Four Year Analysis of Residential Lending in Chicago and its Suburbs*, Woodstock Institute, Chicago, 1986.

General

Ball, M., Harloe, M., Martens, M. *Housing and Social Change in Europe and America*, Routledge, New York and London, 1988 (paperback edn. 1990)

Eurostat 7, Office du Publications Officielles des Communautês Europeênes, Luxembourg, 1989.

Harloe, M. *Private Rental Housing in America and Europe*, Croom Helm, Beckenham, 1985.

Harloe, M., Martens, M. 'Innovation in contemporary housing markets' in Turner, B. et al. (eds) *Between State and Market: Housing in the Post-Industrial Era*, Almqvist and Wicksell, Stockholm, 1987.

UN Statistical Yearbook 1985/6, New York, United Nations, 1988.